Conversation Classrooms

Conversation Classrooms

A Profound Shift from Delivery of Information to Partnership

2nd Edition

Frank Thoms

ROWMAN & LITTLEFIELD
Lanham • Boulder • New York • London

Published by Rowman & Littlefield
An imprint of The Rowman & Littlefield Publishing Group, Inc.
4501 Forbes Boulevard, Suite 200, Lanham, Maryland 20706
www.rowman.com

86-90 Paul Street, London EC2A 4NE

Copyright © 2024 by Frank Thoms

All rights reserved. No part of this book may be reproduced in any form or by any electronic or mechanical means, including information storage and retrieval systems, without written permission from the publisher, except by a reviewer who may quote passages in a review.

British Library Cataloguing in Publication Information Available

Library of Congress Cataloging-in-Publication Data

Names: Thoms, Frank, 1938– author.
Title: Conversation classrooms : a profound shift from delivery of information to partnership / Frank Thoms.
Other titles: Teaching that matters
Description: 2nd edition. | Lanham, Maryland : Rowman & Littlefield, [2023]
Identifiers: LCCN 2023041155 (print) | LCCN 2023041156 (ebook) |
  ISBN 9781475871388 (cloth) | ISBN 9781475871395 (paperback)
  | ISBN 9781475871401 (ebook)
Subjects: LCSH: Teaching. | Learning, Psychology of. | Thought and thinking—Study and teaching. | Conversation.
Classification: LCC LB1025.3 .T533 2023 (print) | LCC LB1025.3 (ebook) | DDC 371.102—dc23/eng/20230914
LC record available at https://lccn.loc.gov/2023041155
LC ebook record available at https://lccn.loc.gov/2023041156

*I dedicate this book to my remarkable eighth graders,
to my seven-to-ten-year-old cherubs in Oxfordshire, England,
to my beloved Russians who were seeking
life's freedom in the Gorbachev years,
and to the teachers I was privileged to teach.*

Conversation (n)

(1) : oral exchange of sentiments, observations, opinions, or ideas
 // . . . we had talk enough but no conversation;
 there was nothing discussed
   —Samuel Johnson

(2) : an instance of such an exchange:
 // a quiet conversation

—Merriam-Webster

When you grow up you tend to get told the world is the way it is and your life is just to live your life inside the world. Try not to bash into the walls too much. Try to have a nice family life, have fun, save a little money.

That's a very limited life. Life can be much broader once you discover one simple fact, and that is—everything around you that you call life, was made up by people that were no smarter than you. And you can change it, you can influence it, you can build your own things that other people can use.

The minute that you understand that you can poke life and actually something will, you know if you push in, something will pop out the other side, that you can change it, you can mold it. That's maybe the most important thing. It's to shake off this erroneous notion that life is there and you're just gonna live in it, versus embrace it, change it, improve it, make your mark upon it.

I think that's very important and however you learn that, once you learn it, you'll want to change life and make it better, cause it's kind of messed up, in a lot of ways. Once you learn that, you'll never be the same again.

—Steve Jobs, *One Last Thing*

Contents

Foreword   xiii
   Anthony T. Polito

Acknowledgments   xvii

Introduction   1

PART I: CONVERSATIONS: THE CENTER OF SUCCESSFUL SCHOOLS   7

Chapter 1: On Mentoring: Unlock the Door to Collaboration   9

Chapter 2: On Dialogue: Be Open to One Another   11

Chapter 3: On Coaching: Provide Nonjudgmental Support   15

Chapter 4: On Lessons: Stimulate Thinking and Retention   19

Chapter 5: On Recruiting: Make Schools Safe   23

Chapter 6: On Phones: Regarding Their Merit for the Classroom   27

Chapter 7: On Sabbaths: Put Aside Electronic Devices   31

Chapter 8: On Portals: Expand the Reach of the Classroom   35

PART II: REFLECTIONS: PONDERING POSSIBILITIES   37

Chapter 9: On Conversation: Invoke Reflective Talking and Listening   39

Chapter 10: On Macro Keys: Apply Technology to Improve Writing   43

Chapter 11: On Metaphor: Put Student Learning First   47

Chapter 12: On the Four Agreements: Find Your Center   51

PART III: INSIGHTS: THE WISDOM OF CONTEMPLATING IDEAS — 55

Chapter 13: On the Bystander: Choose Non-action — 57

Chapter 14: On Lesson Plans: Focus on Learning — 59

Chapter 15: On Everything Has Its Own Speed: Don't Kill the Butterfly — 63

Chapter 16: On PowerPoint: See the Emperor Not Wearing Any Clothes — 67

Chapter 17: On Symphony: Teach to the Whole Child — 69

Chapter 18: On Being at the Center: Discover the Internet as a Metaphor for the Universe — 73

Chapter 19: On Brain Research: Seek Applications for the Classroom — 77

Chapter 20: On Examining Practice: Provide Choices — 81

PART IV: LETTER WRITING: THE POWER OF PAUSE — 85

Chapter 21: Letter to Alicia: Celebrate Your Uniqueness — 87

Chapter 22: Letter to Pamela: Make Partnerships Your Priority — 91

Chapter 23: Letter to Peter: Be Yourself — 95

PART V: BUILDING TRUST AND RESPECT: A PLAN FOR BETTER SCHOOLS — 99

Chapter 24: See It, Say It, Fix It: Rethink Teaching — 101

Chapter 25: Replace Factory-Model Schools: Eliminate Crippling Hierarchies — 105

Chapter 26: Invoke a New Paradigm: Make Trust and Respect the Centerpiece — 111

Coda — 117

Notes — 119

About the Author — 125

Foreword

Anthony T. Polito

Working as an educational administrator for over thirty years, I was never able to have dessert. I led with the appetizer, the endless planning meetings in preparation for major initiatives we were about to unveil. I partook of the entrée, as well, the implementation of the initiatives, observations, data gathering, and the resultant endless tweaking.

But, I was never able to savor the dessert, the celebration of what my colleagues and I accomplished for students, parents, and teachers. Because of the demands of the appetizers and entrées, I could not enjoy the fruits of success. I was on the way to burnout.

Until I met Frank Thoms.

Frank became my ally on the pathway to the dessert I so needed. I first met him in 2000 as a new assistant superintendent. At that point in my career, I had been a teacher and principal for almost twenty-five years in both public and private schools. Without ever having my dessert, I worried about sustaining my enthusiasm as a central office administrator.

In my new district, I became responsible for the professional development of teachers. When Frank arrived, we shared stories, mine about my administrative career, his about his passionate years in the classroom. Together we assessed the needs of the district and drew up plans. The longer we worked together, the more I could begin to smell the dessert. Frank helped me understand what works and what does not and that success is not an accident.

We developed a series of workshops and courses for the district's new teachers, mentors, and veteran staff. He designed innovative programs tailored to our curriculum needs. He also delivered keynotes at the beginning of the new school year. He became a friend and confidant to our teachers.

When I moved on as an administrator in other districts, Frank and I maintained our relationship. We planned courses, workshops, and keynotes. For the past ten years, I have been a superintendent and have kept close ties with Frank. He has implemented innovative programs in differentiated instruction, standards-based curriculum, new teacher workshops, classroom management, workshops on standards for high school faculty—and led Socratic-style seminars for me and my administrative team.

For what seems like over one hundred hours of collaboration in classrooms, in schools, over the phone, at workshops, and even dinners in restaurants when there was no room left in the workday, Frank helped me become a better educator. Now in my work where I still provide the appetizer and the entrée, I can now enjoy the dessert. I maintain my zest and vitality for what some call "God's work."

And that's what this book is all about: maintaining the same wondrous curiosity for learning, for ourselves as well as for our students, which makes the acquisition of knowledge, skills, and understandings—and a love of learning—the real dessert of life.

Frank Thoms was gifted early on in his career with an understanding about what matters in teaching, what most of us do not realize until our teaching careers are nearly over. Because the task of teaching is so complex, we plow forward with our heads down and miss the forest for the trees. For many of us, our eureka moment arrives as we decide to start moving up the administrative ladder, or unfortunately for others of us, as we leave education altogether.

Frank discovered his first eureka moment in his second year of teaching. At that time, most teachers were teaching from a podium at the front of the room, where students sat in rows, and were allowed virtually no opinion or options regarding what would take place during the lesson. These teachers created over 90 percent of the sound in the classroom.

In his social studies classroom, Frank brought student learning to a much higher level beyond simple recall. He knew he was breaking new ground. Some colleagues greeted his experiments with great skepticism. In his introduction, Frank gives superb examples of his ingenuity throughout his nearly forty-year career in catalyzing students to high levels of creativity. He consistently asked students to become more responsible for what happens in the classroom—and for their own learning.

Despite school reform efforts in the past one hundred years, significant bastions of resistance still allow students to fail because they are just plain bored and unmotivated. The most egregious resistance is the inability of many schools to recognize the cultural changes that have arisen from the explosion of technology in the culture. Yet, like it or not, digital technology is washing over our schools and classrooms.

Some districts have dumped textbooks entirely and substituted them with notebooks, laptops, and iPads. Here Frank is again ahead of the curve. I would make Frank's chapter "On Sabbaths: Put Aside Electronic Devices" required reading for all teachers and administrators. In this chapter, we learn that we must make our peace with the fast-changing digital culture—and in fact embrace it. Yet at the same time, we must understand that it cannot become the tyrant that dictates what we do in the classroom.

Just like the old blackboard and chalk, Frank respects digital devices as tools. Many of us have heard the expression that God speaks to us when there is silence. When we choose to turn off electronic devices, we allow our innate intelligence and creativity to speak to us as lifelong learners.

Conversation Classrooms: A Profound Shift from Delivery of Information to Partnership matters. It matters to teachers and administrators. It matters to educational planners, like state legislators steeped in accountability who, in their insistence on nonstop assessments, forget what most students need. And, it matters to students who deserve an engaged education.

We need to help students make sense of our educational system and understand why they are there. We need to help them appreciate school as a collaborative place where they have a role in what and how they learn. We need to show them that reaching their highest educational potential is a function of being able to have choice in what they do in the classroom—and that learning is indeed the dessert of life.

Anthony T. Polito
Educational Consultant, former Superintendent of Schools,
Athol-Royalston Regional School District

Acknowledgments

I want to acknowledge first those special teachers who led me to become a teacher and writer. Miss Karasack in the fourth grade, the tallest person in my world then, had patience with my insistence on taking shortcuts; Miss Mason in the sixth, shorter and teary-eyed, allowed for emotion, especially when she read aloud Longfellow's *Evangeline*.

Thomas Donovan, cantankerous and brilliant, challenged me to learn two years of French in one; Charlie Keller, beloved family friend and professor, encouraged me to become a teacher; Orville Murphy, a history professor who saw my real potential as a student; Sidney Eisen, another history professor, who trusted my abilities at a difficult time that allowed me to stay in college.

In graduate school, Reginald Archambault, preeminent teacher and philosopher, taught me to seek my own answers. Later in graduate school again, Vincent Rogers steered me to Oxfordshire for one my most memorable years of teaching; Philo T. Pritzkau, archetypical professor of philosophy, taught me and my classmates to see and understand everything as it is.

I am indebted to my first students upon whose shoulders I began pursuing my dream—and to each and every student since then with whom I've been blessed to have taught and learned from. Without students, teachers cannot teach; without mine, I would not have become the teacher I was. And I am especially indebted to three mentors: Delmar Goodwin, Barrie Rodgers, and David Mallery. Creative, persistent, compassionate men.

Now as a writer, I have been encouraged by wonderful people over the years. Many have stayed with me from my earliest efforts. Jill Mirman's advice and counsel enriched my thinking and supported my ideas. John D'Auria, president of Teachers21, encouraged my efforts both as a consultant as well as a writer. And, of course, my dear friend Barbara Barnes, my friend and colleague for more than fifty years, was beside me throughout that time.

In San Miguel de Allende, Mexico, where I've been writing for more than ten years, Ken Morrow, Lynn Learned, Sharon Steeber, Linda Laino, Tasha

Paley, Cami Sands, Chet Kozlowski, and others have offered added critical insights to my writing process.

And last but certainly not least, my wife, Kathleen Cammarata, has offered insights and inspired me to persist no matter what.

Frank Thoms
San Miguel de Allende, Mexico
October 2023

Introduction

> Good teaching is the art of creating the content of a thoughtful conversation.
>
> —Joseph Featherstone[1]

Teachers are leaving classrooms in droves. Countless classrooms either have no adult in the room or have someone hired to babysit. Children are being shortchanged. Many blame Covid for this crisis, but evidence of the exodus of discontented teachers began well before. And since Covid, pressures from culture wars from the right have compounded the situation.

I have chosen to write a second edition for *Teaching that Matters: Engaging Minds, Improving Schools*, because I want to provide twenty-first-century teachers with hope amid the present chaos. Without hope, despair reigns. With hope, darkness dissipates. Mired in despair, we become entrapped and pessimistic. With hope, we sense who we are and believe what we are doing will make a positive difference.

We teach because we care. We enter the profession, most of us I believe, because we want to provide children an education that provides knowledge, wisdom, and understanding. We need all the help and support possible. It is why I am writing.

For the second edition of *Teaching that Matters*, I have chosen a new title: *Conversation Classrooms: A Profound Shift from Delivery of Information to Partnership*. Through conversations, you who are in the classroom can build partnerships with your students—and students will partner with one another. No longer will you come to class with an agenda that delivers information for students to receive and later return on quizzes and tests. Instead, you will see yourself on a bridge where you bring information to share that invites thinking, wondering, questioning, ideas, respect. Where experience is the center of your classroom, where mutual understanding is intrinsic, everyone free to express ideas, everyone having the right to speak, and everyone listens. You and your students will be learning together in a democratic classroom.

In its twenty-six short chapters, *Conversation Classrooms* invites you to reconsider your practice. Some chapters provide insight into rethinking common practices with an eye toward making them more accessible. Others offer innovative ideas from unlikely sources. All of them provide hope for your classroom to become dynamic, rigorous, friendly, and compassionate.

I advocate that the conversation metaphor for teaching practice is fundamental to education. When you choose to enter into partnerships with your students, you shift away from one-way teaching. You and your students experience ideas together on equal playing field. You are educating each other. You arrange your room, when possible, so your students can see one another and not the backs of heads.

You choose to listen as much or more than you talk. Everyone is engaged and pays attention to everyone. Everyone's thoughts belong. A democratic classroom mindset emerges. Passivity stays outside. Your students leave class remembering what was exchanged instead of going home to do worksheets or study notes.

In a conversation classroom, students arrive wondering what might happen. You arrive with a plan but understand that something else might transpire. Thinking becomes more important than absorbing. Experiencing liveliness in learning leads to reflection and builds retention. Your classroom may be the last vestige of hope in the culture for holding face-to-face conversations without distractive social media devices. This is important.

The chapters in *Conversation Classrooms* stimulate conversations among colleagues at meetings, perhaps even in the staff room and after school. Given the open-ended quality of topics, they could be used to set an agenda for discussion and will contribute to better and more informed teaching throughout the school.

Conversations have been a part of human civilization since early man held them around campfires. Communities holding conversations where deliberative thinking predominates, especially in today's polarized society, combat the influx of soundbites, misinformation, and disinformation.

Education is not about treating the brain as a vessel to be filled. It is not about asking for regurgitation of what's been delivered. To educate, from the Latin *educere*, means to lead out, to lead forth. Each day different. Each class different. Some groups are naturally curious, others ask lots of questions, and others remain quiet. Some students "get it," others struggle. And each day is a new day, a new opportunity to learn and think—for students and teacher. And an opportunity for students and teachers to know themselves better.

I offer *Conversation Classrooms* as a gift. I recognize that teachers are overworked with little time for settling in to read books. The chapters in sections I–IV, with few exceptions, take about ten to fifteen minutes to read and process. Each offers specific insights and strategies that invite engagement and encourage the classroom to be a place with learning at its hub. The three chapters in part V are longer and are focused on radical changes necessary for schools to become learning centers rather than conveyor belts putting out students with transcripts and résumés.

I hope this book will give you permission to act as the teacher you want and need to be. You did not come into the profession to someone else's bidding. You came to be yourself. Your students will thank you for it.

WHO AM I AND WHY AM I WRITING TO YOU?

I was a twentieth-century teacher, who mostly taught in a public middle school—with a few years in a private school—and was a consultant to teachers for twelve years in the early twenty-first century. I also was an assistant master in a progressive primary school in England. I taught English to Russians from seven to seventeen in four Soviet schools in the Gorbachev era, and three years after the fall of the Soviet Union I led a seminar for Russian teachers coming to America. And I have taught briefly in San Miguel de Allende, Mexico, where I now live.

I was fortunate to be the teacher I wanted to be. I developed my own curricula. I created varied and deep learning experiences. I invited students to make choices in their learning. And I clearly acknowledge that in writing this book I have been away from the classroom for many years and away from the myriad of contemporary challenges teachers now face.

Let me share examples of the kind of teaching I have done in my career. From my first years in the early 1960s I chose to be an innovative teacher. In my second year at a junior/senior high school, I moved from teaching European history with textbooks in the ninth grade to the eighth, where I was responsible for designing an area studies course on South Africa, South America, and Russia and the Soviet Union. For the Russian unit, I dispensed with textbooks, secured material from the Soviet Embassy in Washington, and collected primary source materials. I chose to teach Marxist-Communism as legitimate ideologies, not as evil dogmas, so my students would take them seriously.

Pulling the shades on my windows and blocking the clear-glass panel on my door, I spent a week proclaiming the virtues of Marxist-Engels principles. We turned the room into a Soviet classroom with a Cossack mural over the blackboard, bulletin boards with students' work demonstrating the virtues of Communism, and a diorama with Nikita Khrushchev at the back. In using stick-figure diagrams and holding volatile question-answer sessions, I invited my students to internalize the virtues of the enemy's ideology. I reinforced it by having them spend a day dressed in Soviet-school garb and emulated learning the Soviet way. And we read the *Communist Manifesto*.

Ten years later, after a year of teaching in an exemplary Oxfordshire, England, open-plan progressive primary school, I returned home to establish a sixth-seventh-eighth-grade open classroom. I was fascinated with the idea of working alongside fellow teachers to provide opportunities for students to become drivers of their own education—inside our rigorous expectations.

For social studies, I improvised the board game Diplomacy,[2] which had been designed for two to seven players and simulated it into a class-wide activity involving twenty-plus students that lasted more than a month. "Diplomats" engage in intensive negotiations before making "moves" on the board; creating multiple "alliances" between countries; making secret "agreements"; and preparing "propaganda" posters that were scattered throughout the classroom. The game concluded with a Diplomacy dinner, in which some students (most of whom were not involved in the game) designed a menu based on different European cuisines and did all the cooking and serving.

Another innovation from that time was restructuring the board game Monopoly into a socialist version, Co-opoly. The rules specified that players were to play for an equal (at least equitable) share of money and real estate. It was a challenge but proved intriguing. I listened in on surprising conversations.

Later, in the mid-1980s when teaching social studies in a four-person team, I continued to teach about Russia and the USSR. Meanwhile, Gorbachev's *glasnost* tempted Americans like myself to travel to the Soviet Union and to meet the "enemy" behind the Iron Curtain. I jumped at the chance and ended up taking eight adventurous trips from 1985 to 1994, three of which included service as a teacher of English in four Soviet schools in Leningrad, Moscow, and Alma Ata, Kazakhstan.

Returning home from my first trips, I focused on having my students understand its history as realistically as possible. I was tired of reading Soviet propaganda, its braggadocio to the rest of the world about its space spectaculars, military might, and expanding nuclear arsenal. And I disdained reading anti-Soviet chapters in textbooks and listening to US pundits take potshots at Russians. I wanted to penetrate that wall and go behind it and meet real Russians.[3]

I invoked George Orwell's *Animal Farm* to probe the Soviet mindset and its modes of operation. Yet, Orwell never mentions Russia or the Soviet Union. I assigned students to read one chapter per night and not to read ahead. After each chapter, we speculated on what would happen next. This approach made for stimulating conversations. After finishing the book, the *pièce de résistance* was offering students the option to reenter the book at any part and rewrite it in a way that they saw fit.

One of the favorite choices turned out to be "Chapter XI," a postscript to Orwell's final chapter, "Chapter X." Its infamous quotation, "The creatures outside looked from pig to man, and from man to pig, and from pig to man again; but already it was impossible to say which was which,"[4] was an obvious entry into another chapter. What my students envisioned may not have satisfied Orwell, but they did represent original thinking in well-written essays.

My final incarnation teaching about Russians and the Soviets happened with eighth graders in a private school in the 1990s, my last decade in the classroom. For one unit, we spent considerable time examining the plight of peasants during the reign of Ivan IV. I asked students to take on roles in Russian society and draft petitions on behalf of peasants to present to the tsar.

After thorough research and intense class discussions, students prepared authentic-looking parchment petitions laced with burnt edges. When they delivered their petitions to Ivan IV, "the Terrible" (a colleague disguised as the tsar), they approached reverently, dropping to their knees. The combination of authentic-looking petitions, well-researched information, and dressing as peasants and nobles to face the tsar (and never turning their backs on him) put them deep into early Russian history.

By no means did I limit myself to Marxism-Communism, Russian history, and the Soviet era. When I taught ancient history, my students and I explored the wisdom of Confucius, Lao Tzu, and the Buddha in ancient China. It was an intense experience in which we investigated the analects of Confucius, the wisdom of the Tao, and writings of Buddhists.

Not only did my students probe Confucian analects and chapters from Lao Tzu's *Tao Te Ching*, I invited them write their own, which proved far more worthy than taking tests. For the final project, I invited them to "travel" to China as eighth graders to bring back wisdom to their socially struggling community. And so they did!

Throughout my career, I made every effort to engage students' minds, encouraged them to do their best, and invited them to express their knowledge in rigorous and creative ways. These examples of breaking traditional patterns of teaching from the front of the room illustrate that teaching can be a creative process with endless possibilities. It was the only way I knew how to teach. It's the reason I am now a writer.

Since I've left teaching, I am compelled to reach out to today's teachers, to you who are "in the trenches." I have published five books and now this one. I believe the least I can do is offer what I've learned over my fifty years. I hope it helps.

REFLECTION/ACTION

How might you use the first two pages of the introduction to explore the importance of conversations in the classroom and among teachers and administrators? Do you think that it is possible to open education to focus on students' learning rather than completing curricula expectations? Is this unrealistic for educators? For politicians? And can you imagine enacting your own curriculum as described in the second half of the introduction?

PART I

Conversations: The Center of Successful Schools

*Any time two or more people choose to speak
and listen, they are in conversation.*

Whether people recognize it or not, when they are sharing their thoughts and others are listening, they are in a conversation. In this process ideas arise, both in the speaker and in the listener. Where the ideas move to depends upon what people choose. But without a culture of conversation, teachers are likely to stay "where they are," most likely delivering from the front of the room. After all, they may have been doing just that for years. Students come and go, the contract is renewed, and so it goes.

But it in conversations thinking becomes possible. Partnerships can form. At the moment of conversation, everyone is on the same page. When one lectures often from a podium or standing at the front of the room, listeners sit immobile. It signals "one-way" time. Good for a while, but not enough for an education.

Conversation Classrooms is an invitation to consider the importance of two-way relationships: between teachers and students, teachers and administration—between all parties. In this section, readers witness exchanges mostly between teachers and a few with principals. All the conversations happen with students in mind.

Chapter 1

On Mentoring

Unlock the Door to Collaboration

> *Critical Friends Groups enable mentors and new teachers to move beyond their confidential relationship and improve teaching and learning—not only for themselves but also for their colleagues.*

When Principal Victoria Roberts asked Claire Fox-Rogan, a fifth-year teacher of social studies, if she was willing to mentor a new teacher in her department, Claire was more than pleased. She had navigated her first year alone before her school had a mentor program. She remembers how she found help when there was no mentor program. She confided in other new teachers, colleagues in her department, and occasionally with her vice principal. She was pleased that they were willing to help, because they understood the challenges facing new teachers.

She became an advocate for mentoring by arguing how difficult it had been for her and her fellow new colleagues without it. She recognized that her school's culture, like most, expected teachers to be on their own in their classrooms. One respected veteran would not allow anyone into her room when she was teaching; because of her strong reputation, no one challenged her.

The practice of classroom privacy enabled teachers to be unaccountable, except, of course, to their students. Claire thought that a mentoring program would crack open the issue of privacy and provide needed support. And as important, mentoring new teachers would encourage them to stay in teaching.

Mentoring is a relationship between two people with the goal of professional and personal development. It works best when the parameters of the relationship are clear. Claire and her protégé, Drew Cummings, met in confidence; with agreement from Drew, she sought out other teachers on the staff to help him and spoke to administration, if necessary, but only with Drew's knowledge.

But Claire believed that a mentoring program, as good as it might be, would not resolve a prevailing predicament endemic in her school—and in other schools: teachers having to be alone in their classrooms throughout the day. Mentoring breaks this isolation but is only a beginning. Real collaboration among teachers is indispensable for a good school, she thought—and would take time to implement.

When at a conference, she learned about Critical Friends Groups®, a doorway to collaboration that has been successful for more than twenty-five years. Its protocol advocates that "Friends," comprised of five to twelve educators, commit to meet for two hours at least once a month, the purpose being to improve students' achievement. Some groups have certified CFG coaches.[1]

The value of this protocol, Claire grasped, is that teachers address problems with colleagues and administrators without fear of being judged. Having conversations about their ideas and challenges builds close partnerships. Everyone has the same goal: to improve student learning.

The extended value of CFGs is that they open classrooms to one another. No longer do teachers have to work without feedback. Education becomes a collaborative process. It is not *congeniality*—teachers are good at that—but true *collegiality*, sharing responsibility with one another, which is more challenging but essential. And supervisors who join CFGs look for potential in teachers and participate in nourishing it; "going public" becomes common practice.

As a result, the isolated classroom becomes an anomaly—for protégés, for mentors, and for members of the CFG, and hopefully throughout the school. Collaboration breaks the cycle of teachers teaching alone. New teachers will learn that collegiality is the foundation of successful teaching. Having conversations builds self-confidence. In this paradigm, the odds are that fewer new teachers will drop out, whereas now nearly 50 percent leave the profession in their first five years. Having new teachers stay is what Claire hopes for.

REFLECTION/ACTION

Teaching is complex. You need one another's support to meet the myriad of challenges you now face both in the classroom and from outside. Doing it alone is no longer viable; think about that. Commit to mentoring a young teacher whether or not your school has a formal program. Be there for that teacher. Advocate for a Critical Friends Group to anyone who will listen. Or form one on your own, a hybrid version if necessary.

Chapter 2

On Dialogue

Be Open to One Another

> *When teachers welcome colleagues and administrators to work alongside them, everyone gains, which nourishes positive change.*

After language arts department meetings, Sally Walters, a reflective, thoughtful seventh-grade teacher, would often ponder about her teaching and her role in the school. She wanted her classes to be memorable. One day on her way home, she wondered why most teachers seemed to be reluctant to have colleagues and administrators observe their teaching. Other professions depended on collaboration including doctors, lawyers, businesses, aviators, and social workers. While she liked having her domain, she learned early on how important it is to receive feedback. And she has been baffled by the habit of having scheduled principal's evaluations of teachers, which she feels lead only to dog and pony shows.

If our schools are going to improve, she thought, we need to have conversations. We need to move beyond our isolated rooms, each doing our own thing. We need to observe one another. Most of what she learned about others' practices came from rumors she heard in the staff room.

How can we break this cycle? What holds us back from seeking feedback from colleagues and administrators? Why are we afraid of administrator visits? Why are administrators hesitant to visit? Why have colleagues preferred scheduled dog-and-pony-show evaluations to assure that they will be seen at their best?

To open up this can of worms, Sally asked her principal, Arthur Prince, if she could present an idea at the next faculty meeting to break the pattern of isolation. Surprisingly, he agreed with her idea. When it was her turn to speak at the meeting, she shared a story about Benjamin Zander, a professor at a conservatory. Zander missed his opportunity to teach, because his students played perfectly whenever he was present—a dog and pony show. And his grading system was based on performance.

"Zander wanted to breakdown this grade barrier," Sally began. "He wanted to be free to become their teacher. He came up with the idea to have his students write a letter to him in the past tense dated at the end of the term explaining how they earned their As. Once they passed in their letter, they no longer needed to be concerned about their grade. They could play pieces in front of him with squeaks, missed notes, et al. He was then able to offer feedback—to be a teacher. And if he ever saw one of his musicians not acting as an A student, he reminded her of her commitment.

"Grading is an issue all of us struggle with," Sally continued. "Whereas a 4.0 grade average used to be rare, now many earn 4.0+. Students and their parents pressure us to give As, and our school's reputation depends on students getting into good colleges. While I do not think we could use Zander's letter approach with our students, with different approaches, I believe we can apply his idea among ourselves.

"I want to invite each of you, my colleagues," Sally concluded, "to consider writing a letter to your supervisors in which you describe your personal expectations as teachers." She projected an example of such a letter on the screen:

> As you can see from the expectations that I've placed on myself, I want you to know me as an accomplished teacher. I have high standards for what I want my students to learn. But I need help in taking them there. Teaching is difficult. I hope you will be willing to take time to come into my room and be alongside me and my students. I try my best, but I would do better if you are there to provide feedback. Our conversations will give both of us food for thought.
>
> You have been willing to listen when we come to you with problems. At faculty meetings you offer good ideas. And, your experience as a teacher gives you a good perspective on what we do. I hope you will join me in improving my students' learning.

Sally opened a door. Such a letter could lead to a leveling of the playing field: the teacher and supervisor working together toward making a better classroom. When the supervisor arrives, together they will be focusing on how well students are learning. Collaboration is in place. Conversations follow. Sally suggests that teachers consider doing the same for each other. And when the principal visits, he comes to support what has been happening.

Sally's colleagues appreciated her taking the initiative to address them at a faculty meeting. Usually only administrators and department heads delivered messages. Her comments generated a lively and productive conversation. She was pleased. And some decided then and there to write a letter to their supervisor; speaking up for themselves was something most hadn't thought about.

Over the weekend, Sally thought about Benjamin Zander's letter. She wanted to try his approach with her students but would have to take a different tack. She decided to ask them to write a letter to her dated at the end of the month, stating reasons for getting the grade they think they would deserve for that month. The real value of the letter was not the grade itself; the process of writing the letter would become the centerpiece, students having to reflect on their learning, becoming more self-aware, more proactive, and having conversations about it.

Sally was grateful that being a teacher offered her opportunities to explore and experiment by being open to her students, to their thoughts and emotions. Having conversations gave them agency, and in turn she learned from them. She understood that she would be in partnership with them every day, in every class. And she learned at the faculty meeting that conversations with her colleagues would keep them in partnership.

REFLECTION/ACTION

Assess your relationship with your department head or supervisor. How can you make it better? You could choose to write a letter in the spirit Sally has suggested. And you could invite students into a similar process by implementing her approach (or your own). Each of these actions, teacher with supervisor and teacher with students, open all parties to making choices—essential to education.

Chapter 3

On Coaching

Provide Nonjudgmental Support

> *Active feedback from coaches breaks open the perpetual isolation of the classroom and provides teachers with support and ideas.*

Ann Norton keeps her teaching voice with her sixth graders at a fever pitch. The closer to making a point the louder she becomes. By the end of the class, her shrill speech resonates. Tall and well dressed, she is positive, friendly, competent, open, energetic, supportive, caring—and loud.

Tony Palermo, principal of a new charter school, decided to hire Rod Trainer, an experienced consultant whom he respected and who was known for his empathy for beginning teachers. Rod had been a middle school science teacher before he became a consultant. His colleagues respected him.

In his first year as a consultant, Rod led a dozen after-school workshops for new teachers in several schools. The next year, in addition to giving workshops at Tony's middle school, Tony asked him to visit classrooms, observe each new teacher for a class period, and offer insights to improve practice. Rod knows that these teachers, like most, spend nearly all their time alone with students.

When he sat down with Ann Norton, he had no difficulty opening the conversation. "Ann, what are your thoughts about today's lesson?"

"It was pretty typical of what I do each day. The school expects us to keep up with the schedule we have each week. I focus on the task at hand and do what I can do to stay on pace. What do you think?"

"For a first-year teacher," Rod replied, "you have command of your subject matter. Your introduction to fractions and the paragraph-writing segments were well structured. You appear to know your students well and responded effectively to each of them. As for Juan, who you've said has been difficult, you kept him engaged; he did not act out.

"You chose to stand up front for nearly all the period. You kept everyone's attention using popsicle sticks to assure that each student had an opportunity to participate."

(Rod hesitated to bring up the issue of her voice. He felt she might take it personally. But he wanted her to know that he was there to help her, not evaluate her. He broached the subject cautiously but directly.)

"Ann, have you noticed during the period that your voice becomes louder?"

"Oh, I've never thought about that."

"Yes, you become quite loud. My concern is if you stay at a high pitch, you could hurt or possibly damage your vocal cords. I learned from a colleague early on in my teaching that lowering your voice can keep the attention of your students. Some teachers have suggested that when you whisper, students strain to hear you. I don't suggest that you do that, but I am saying that lowering your voice should work better for you—and for them."

"Come to think of it, my throat feels very hoarse at the end of the day. I will give your suggestion a try. Thank you."

"You're welcome."

A month later Rod returned to the school for a workshop with Ann and the other new teachers. Ann spoke about her decision to quiet her voice. "It took several days for me and my students to get used to my lower voice, but now we have!"

Ann had made a breakthrough, not only about an aspect of her teaching but also about her power to change practice. Without Rod's feedback, she may not have become conscious of her rising voice level until her throat started to suffer. Now she could modulate it and create a positive effect on her students—and on herself. She realized, too, how much better her throat felt at the end of the day.

"Once you realize that you are the one who decides how you teach," Rod said to the group, "you do not have to teach as you currently do or as you think you're supposed to. Pay attention to what works and what does not and feel free to change. And, if you open your room to colleagues and administrators to observe and share with you what they notice, all the better. You may have bad habits waiting to be discovered and needing change, much to the relief of your students—and to you!"

As teachers, we work in a vacuum. Often, the only feedback we receive comes when supervisors evaluate us, usually on scheduled visits, which can become dog and pony shows where we are at our best (we want to keep our contract); our administrator may also be wanting to see that all is well and not have to worry about you.

When we're new, we would be fortunate to have a mentor, an instructional coach, or a colleague observing us "teaching for real." Having conversations about our teaching without judgment frees us to reinforce what is working and to discover new methods.

We could also seek responses from students. We could use classroom response systems (clickers), which provide information during lessons about what students are thinking—and assure anonymity at the same time. And we could use phones for feedback when we have them in the classroom for instructional purposes.

At the end of class, we could invoke a tried-and-true practice of exit cards with prompts: "What I learned today"; "What I need help with"; or exit tickets where students at the end of the period solve a problem or answer a question to see how they grasped the lesson. And to save time, put homework assignments on the class website.

We can break out of our self-imposed tyranny of the isolated classroom. We can find colleagues and administrators who are willing to have respectful conversations that lead to partnerships to improve our teaching. And, if fortunate, we will have instructional coaches to nurture our growth.

"No man is an island," John Donne wrote. No one is self-sufficient; everyone relies on others. The same is true for teachers.

REFLECTION/ACTION

Are you alone in your classroom? Think about what a difference it would make to have a colleague or instructional coach in your room. How could you make that happen? Education is better for everyone with collaboration inside the classroom as well as throughout the school. And one obvious source: include formative feedback from students, but for obvious reasons, don't rely only on end-of-the-year evaluations.

Chapter 4

On Lessons

Stimulate Thinking and Retention

When teachers create conversational lessons, they allow surprises to emerge for students and for them.

Musad Amur, a ninth-grade world history teacher, loved his work. His students spoke well of him; they knew he cared about them. He was eager to have them learn. In a conversation with his colleague, Chuck Borgen, Musad expressed frustration. "My students and I get along and they seem to like my class. Every day I prepare careful lectures and deliver them with energy and pizzazz. They listen and take notes, but they are not doing well on tests. I want them to do better."

Chuck listened and wondered how he could help. He was impressed with Musad's self-assessment. He decided to invite Musad to observe his classroom. The next afternoon, Musad watched as Chuck used a variety of approaches during his lesson. Students were active and asked lots of questions. Musad began to think that his strict lecture approach needed revision. Perhaps he had been more focused on what *he* had to say than what *his students* needed from him.

Musad and Chuck met that afternoon in the library after school. Over the course of their conversation, Chuck shared an idea he hoped Musad would appreciate. "In 1983—yes, Musad, 1983—researcher Mary Budd Rowe, published the results of her 10–2 structure idea for teaching: When a teacher decides to lecture, at ten-minute intervals he provides two-minute process breaks, in which students either reflect on their own or talk among themselves in a variety of formats. They can't ask questions to the teacher except in the last five minutes; Budd Rowe wanted students to learn to depend on one another. At the end of class," Chuck concluded, "they will have internalized much of the information from the lecture."[1]

Musad immediately understood this structure's potential but wondered if it would slow his covering the necessary material for the department exam. He thanked Chuck, went home, and decided to give 10–2 a try. For the next several weeks, Musad experimented with a variety of variations, all of which activated his classroom. For the first time in his career, he watched his students think and learn *in* class. And more of them were doing better on quizzes and tests. Somehow—and it was a struggle—he managed to get through enough material to have them ready for the department's exam.

He was opening up to new ways to reach his students. He still prepared careful lectures to provide key information and insights into world history, and he found great pleasure in being alongside his students as they were engaged in the "2" of the 10–2 process. When he introduced the 10–2 structure, some students were confused, others distracted. He tried a variety of possibilities for the two-minute part: giving them a query; having them have a conversation with the person next to them; and other times inviting them to write. Sometimes he would talk for more than ten minutes and would allow the two minutes to stretch into five or six.

Musad transitioned from delivering specific outcomes to focusing on the learning of his students. His newfound lessons stimulated thinking and retention. Most important, his "perfect lecture" included "two-minute" processing segments.

Each day Musad comes into his room with a clear idea of what he wants his students to learn. He has mapped out where he is headed for the week. He has thought about what he wants for the unit, for the term, and for the year. But he remains open as to how to get there—and he discovers surprise landings when they occur. He now relies on his students; together they proceed down "the road less traveled." He trusts their questions, insights, and ideas—and his own as well.

One afternoon after school, he caught up with Chuck in the staff room. "I want to thank you for opening the door to teaching in a two-way classroom. I have never enjoyed teaching so much. Not only do my students appreciate my classes, but they are learning more and doing better on tests—and on the exam! I can't thank you enough."

"I am so pleased, Musad. I am glad we had the conversation about your concerns. I am glad I could help."

After Musad left, Chuck was pleased to have taken the time to help a colleague. He was grateful to have offered to observe Musad and help him improve his practice. And he was looking forward to visiting Musad's classroom. "I wonder what I will discover," Chuck said to himself.

REFLECTION/ACTION

Have you ever asked for help from a colleague? Have you considered offering help? And have you taken the time to pay attention to how much of a class period you spend talking? If it is excessive, incorporate Mary Budd Rowe's 10–2 structure into your teaching. Vary its format to suit your needs. Use it to keep the focus on what your students are learning. Listen to their conversations, not only to what you have to say. Seek feedback from them about their responses. Remember, you and your students are learning together.

Chapter 5

On Recruiting

Make Schools Safe

A school-wide safety net assures that each student belongs.

Liz Ting has wanted to teach since she was five. She played school with her friends, seeing herself as the teacher. She had a natural caring for others. When she role-played teacher, she treated each "student" as if they were special. Now a recent college graduate who double majored in English and education, she can hardly wait to meet her ninth- and eleventh-grade language arts classes.

In workshops for beginning teachers the week before school, she shared that she intended to find ways to engage her students. They all agreed with her on one point: not to replicate traditional ways in which many of their teachers had taught. They were excited to invoke methods to engage students and invite them to conversations to form partnerships; one-way teaching would not be sufficient.

By the third day of school, the optimistic, energetic, and perky Liz was overwhelmed. One hundred twenty-two students and three preps! How could she keep up? She found fellow new teacher Barbara Churner after school in the staff room. Barbara, who taught second grade and was eager to share her love of learning with her students, was also feeling overwhelmed. She spent the whole day with hardly a break with her twenty-nine students *and* having to teach all subjects. "Nobody prepared us for this, did they?"

Despite early frustrations, Liz and Barbara were getting to know their students. Barbara found it easier to learn names, as she had only twenty-nine. Liz, on the other hand, struggled to learn the names of her one hundred twenty-two students; matching names to faces was challenging for her. Like other new teachers, she found herself needing to focus more on her lessons than on individual students.

By the second week, Liz began to see her students less as a group and more as individuals. She was learning their names. Some came easily, particularly those who made themselves known from the first day. But she was surprised on the third day to notice Dan for the first time; he sat at the back of the room in her second period class. She asked herself, *Why haven't I noticed him? How has he been able to slip into the woodwork? How has he avoided me?* Then she remembered learning from a friend the term "gray kids," those who blend in with everyone. Whenever in a group, her friend, a "gray kid" herself, said she had preferred to wait for the right moment to make herself known.[1]

When thinking about Dan, Liz remembered Robert Kegan's research. A Harvard psychologist, Kegan offered a profound perspective that speaks to how teachers perceive students. In his seminal work *The Evolving Self*, he introduced the concept of "recruitability." Hardly anyone can resist a baby's eyes despite the large head, huge forehead, and little body; nature provides them with the natural gift of recruiting. On the other hand, nature is not so kind later on. As people grow older, they do not have equal abilities to recruit. Adolescents are a case in point. Some are more "attractive" than others. Some naturally invite people into their lives while others push people away. And a few slip into the woodwork.

Healthy, well-fed babies in orphanages, Kegan writes, have been known to die when they are deprived of human contact. Making personal connections, apparently, is essential to life. Kegan connects this concept to schools:

> [T]he greatest inequalities in education are not between schools . . . but within them; that greater than the inequalities of social class or achievement test scores is *the unequal capacity of students to interest others in them*—a phenomenon not reducible to social class or intelligence, and which seems to be the more powerful determinant of future thriving.[2]

Kegan asks teachers to recruit—and to be recruitable. They need to be open to all students, not only to those who lure them into their webs but to those who fail to reach out. Schools have to be sure that each and every student is recruited, that each one is looked after by at least one staff person who the student knows and cares for. All students deserve to belong.

How can teachers respond to Kegan's challenge?

New teachers, as Liz discovered, may not be ready to take into account Kegan's recruitability mindset. They are busy trying to claim their space, barely keeping up. They feel pressure to focus on what they need to teach, regardless of knowing that they are supposed to be there for the kids. They struggle to connect with all of them.

As a new teacher, Liz is like a mother sitting beside her child on an airplane. When oxygen masks drop down, as the flight attendant instructs, the mother is to put her mask on first before she puts it on her child. So, too, in the classroom. Liz, who works alone, has to care for herself first, to keep her wholeness amid the chaos of the first days and weeks.

As she becomes more comfortable, she is better able to focus on all of her students—each and every one of them. She's ready to "put their masks on," to recruit them. In Kegan's words, she's ready to level the playing field of "the unequal capacity of students to interest others in them."

Veteran teachers, too, need to take Kegan's insight to heart. Whether they acknowledge it or not, they prefer some students to others; they may say (privately) that they have favorites. Yet they need to take responsibility for recruiting everyone in their classes. Wise teachers recognize that some students who attempt to "hide" in the classroom may be pleading for recognition. Finding a way to connect with those students will bring them into the community—important for them and everyone.

What can schools do?

Ultimately, recruitment is a school-wide responsibility. Brian Flanagan, the flamboyant former principal of Somersworth High School in New Hampshire from 1998 to 2008, developed a system to recruit every student. He required that each teacher who led a club or team become the safety net for those students. He and his vice principal, Carl Fitzgerald, took responsibility for those students not in clubs or on teams. They would have lunch with them. Every student in the school was "recruited." They knew that they belonged.[3]

REFLECTION/ACTION

How well do you know your students? How well does your school know its students? How well does it provide a safety net for each of them? Make sure the administration and your colleagues understand the need to create this safety net. And take time to connect with your students: greet them at the door; ask questions about their lives; watch their games; go to school plays. And let them know who you are, what you care about, value, and your likes and dislikes. Your teaching will thank you.

Chapter 6

On Phones

Regarding Their Merit for the Classroom

Making the classroom a haven away from the constant chatter of connectivity energizes student–teacher interactions and nourishes long-term learning.

In the Sunday comics:

> *Scenario:* A man in a bowler hat with his hands outstretched stands in front of nonsense banners and appeals to a crowd of Pinheads to invite them to come into the big tent behind him.
>
> *First Panel:* "Yes, ladies and gentlemen, they are oddities of nature . . . yet they live among us . . . on the inside! See the man who never looks up from his smartphone! Watch as he collides with furniture and pedestrians!"
>
> *Second Panel:* "See the teenager who never speaks, Yes!! She texts her friends hundreds of times a day . . . even . . . get this . . . when they are standing right next to her!"
>
> *Third Panel:* ". . . and strangest of all, ladies and gentlemen . . . the woman who lives not in the present, but in a timeless limbo of streaming video and photos of herself, constantly uploaded to Facebook, Tumblr and Blogspot! It's all on the inside!"[1]

Bill Griffith's "Zippy the Pinhead" scenario sets the stage for looking in on the lives of today's students. Some come to school with hardly any memory of yesterday's lessons. Every day, they sit with their classmates in one class after another, after another. Then it's on to sports, clubs, and lessons. Then home alone. All day connected to smartphones with texts, tweets, Tumblr,

TikTok, Instagram. . . . The present presses on them only to be forgotten in the next present. Their lives are rushed.

It's a life twentieth-century teachers did not grow up with. We had schedules with spaces in between. Most interactions happened in person with peers or on the telephone. Some were bullies, some bullied. Some were good at school. Others not. We played together on our own. And we had conversations with our parents at dinner.

Students who come to school with little memory of yesterday are reminiscent of the central character in the movie *Memento*. Neil Gabler writes, "unable to remember anything . . . compelled to live moment by moment, without the past ever informing the present. The here and now obliterates the there and then . . . in a society in which the present is unmoored, making anything that happens now far more important than anything that has happened before."[2]

Students live on incessant sound bites. Texting messages-of-the-moment, instantly important, just-past messages dissolving into the ether. What's in front of them counts for everything. Phones do not invite remembering the past. Perhaps that's why more students are not doing their homework. It's simply not on their mind.

Rebecca Lankford's school has been wrestling with the issue of cell phones. A language arts teacher for ten years, Rebecca, a Smith College graduate, is known for her wit, intelligence, and ability to connect with her students. At present, the faculty understands that phones have an impact on teaching but has not come to a consensus about policy. Rebecca has argued for the school to purchase Yondr magnetic packets for students to put phones in upon arriving at school; they get them back at the end of the day.

For teachers, this would be a welcome relief, she thought. No blings. No buzzes. No students at their desks dropping their eyes into their laps. Everyone is in the room, physically and (hopefully) mentally. For emergencies, the PA system is there.

Principal Bob MacArthur, known for his broad-minded approach and willingness to listen, called a faculty meeting to have a conversation about what his school should do with cell phones. Clearly, they were having an almost unimaginable impact on kids (and adults).

Elena Draginova, Rebecca's neighbor in the department, spoke first. A recent émigré from St. Petersburg, Russia, Elena brought her zest and curiosity into the school. "Without the invisible distraction of phones in pockets, or in their hands," she began, "I teach hoping to engage students. But many of them do not know how to converse. With the phones put away, I have their attention. I help them look at each other and me in the eye when speaking.

I teach better. I have put my desks into a circle for that purpose. Seeing the backs of heads for conversations makes no sense when you think about it."

"I don't think we should allow phones in the classroom," said Jenny Tsankova, a proverbial twinkle in her eyes, "because we have Chromebooks." She, too, was a Russian immigrant and was famous for her creative lessons. "We know what Chromebooks do for us—and for the kids. For example, I use them to connect to Kahn Academy, where I derive many of my math lessons."

"But I think," spoke up Rebecca, "we are begging the question if we believe Chromebooks replace the phones. They are not phones, and the students know it. And so do we. Phones have become lifelines for most of us. Apps enable us to gain access to the world, to friends and family, to our music, to our favorite celebrities. At the same time, phones can be addictive. And as important, phones can lure us and our students down rabbit holes of misinformation and disinformation into worlds of alternate realities.

"While I prefer my classes without the phone," Rebecca continued, furring her brow, "I realize that I may be trying to hold back the tidal wave before us. Not to deal with phones, not to be with them with our students, we will be putting our heads in the proverbial sand. It's wishing to go back to another time, another culture, one most of us grew up in. Phones are here to stay. Our students are with them every moment when not in our classes. We will be more responsible if we find a way to include phones in our lessons."

"I have a thought," said Mary Maxwell, a teacher of biology, wise beyond her years and known for her practicality. "We need to think about the phone both as a social media device *and* as an instructional tool. We all know how phones can access the world, to the universe when you think about it. All that information waiting to be tapped into—we keep phones out of the classroom. We need to rethink this."

After much conversation, the faculty came to a compromise. They agreed to require students to place their phones in the Yondr pouch upon coming to school; parents would know to call the office to reach their children. But, when a teacher wanted to use phones for instruction, students could retrieve them. Yet, everyone recognized it would take hard work to have the phones in class without students being tempted to tap into their social media.

"We need to come up with a curriculum to teach students how to use their phones," Mary continued. "It will take time, perhaps much time but necessary. Students (and adults) need to learn to become crap detectors, to learn to know which sites are legitimate and to look with askance at suspicious sites that pop up. It could be the most challenging teaching we will do. The Internet and phones await with countless rabbit holes popping up to lure people." Before the end of the meeting, those faculty savvy with the role of the Internet and phones agreed to come up with approaches to this problem—and soon.

Meanwhile, everyone agreed to have nonjudgmental conversations with students about the difference between phones for instructional purposes and as social media. As soon as students switch to social media, the phone distracts. Students already know this; an obvious example, when they sit at a table with their peers, everyone is on their phone.

REFLECTION/ACTION

Be clear in conversation with your students about your stance on cell phones and, most importantly, listen to their thoughts. Tell them when you will allow cell phones in class, and otherwise, do not. And equally important, have conversations with colleagues with hopes of leading to a school-wide consensus on the role of cell phones in classrooms.

Chapter 7

On Sabbaths

Put Aside Electronic Devices

Taking time away from electronic devices brings solace from daily stress and expands thinking and learning.

After a contentious faculty meeting about the role of phones in classrooms, Eileen Keller turned to her art department colleague, Ford Knight, in the staff room and sighed. "Why can't we come to common ground on this issue? You heard George Mills practically screaming in the meeting insisting that kids be allowed to have their phones on them in class. He clearly believes that since phones are ubiquitous, we do not have a right to restrict students from having them. While he is right about their presence in the culture, I don't believe it means we have to allow them in class. I have a TV in my class, but I don't turn it on all the time. And we certainly do not allow anti-social behavior. Our classroom is our responsibility to make it safe and appealing for learning."

Ford nodded and agreed he preferred to teach without phones. At the same time, he and Eileen realized that the issue could not be ignored. Were they to exclude phones entirely, they would be considered Luddites, especially by their students.

But Ford, who was known for his independent views, offered another question: "Shouldn't we teach about the value of taking sabbaths from the Internet and electronic devices?" He recently read William Powers's short but comprehensive *Hamlet's Blackberry*,[1] published before phones became more in play with people's lives, especially for teenagers. Ford liked Powers's idea of taking "Internet Sabbaths." Perhaps a weekend or one day of the weekend.

"Powers's argument could be applied to phones as well," Ford continued. "Time away from both, from the incessant demands of social media. Time with no interconnectivity. To be in the world, directly, without personal distractions. I think this is important.

"For the past month, I've made Sundays my sabbath from electronic devices. At first, I was anxious about not staying in touch but became used to it. Soon I enjoyed the time away; nothing transpired that I couldn't deal with the next day."

"But there is another matter we should consider," Eileen responded. "Our classrooms may be the one place where students can learn to be together face-to-face without distractions from phones. If they never have this opportunity, they won't learn the joy of conversations, looking one another in the eye, and learning to pay attention to facial expressions, body language, and tone of voice. We might be the last bastion of hope for this to happen."

"Yes, Eileen, I think this is why I love being in the classroom. When we sit in a horseshoe, something I've tried recently, it's even better. My students are beginning to look at one another in the eye (and at me)—and improving their conversation skills. It's been slow, but it's happening!"

Greg McGill, a gregarious, energetic, and popular social studies teacher, had been listening quietly. "You guys, I have been thinking the same thing but from a different angle. I read Nicholas Carr's *The Shallows*[2] several years ago. I learned that not only are classrooms important for learning face-to-face conversations, but they are also important for developing long-term memory.

"Carr quotes Jonathan Sweller, an Australian educational psychologist, who argues that long-term memory is essential if humans are to function effectively. Without it, working memories go on overload, and we become mindless consumers of data. We lose the potential to build on the accomplishments of others."

Greg took a deep breath. "I believe our classrooms are the places where in today's culture students can develop those memories. Where else will they be asked to take extended time away from their electronic devices? Where else will they explore their own minds without device interruptions? Where else will they learn not to google when stuck in their thinking? And where else will they have opportunities to develop essential literacy skills of how to read critically, how to write and rewrite, and how to discuss and argue effectively using evidence? These are even more important now considering the impact of GPT-4.

"Wow, your comments lead me to think that we teachers have an enormous responsibility," said Ford. "I wish everyone on our faculty understood that."

"When in our lessons we ask students to regurgitate what we've told them," Eileen added, "we do not invite thinking. When we allow students to rely on the Internet, they become receptacles rather than creators. Without long-term memories, they will succumb to living in a history-less world, functioning only in the moment. Certainly the Buddha did not intend that 'being in the moment' to mean this."

After talking with Eileen and Ford, Greg thought about the classroom as the savior of face-to-face encounters, as a place to develop long-term thinking—and he and his colleagues as the central actors. He asked himself, *Can we think of becoming partners in conversation with our students and invite them to be free to choose what they think and say? To listen to them? Guide them toward engaged lives?* What a challenge! What a responsibility!

On his way home, he noticed people walking with their heads down immersed in smartphones. Are we becoming a culture in which we no longer look into the faces of those persons passing us by? "Not my choice," he said to himself.

REFLECTION/ACTION

What do you think about taking sabbaths from phones and the Internet? Would you consider taking a half-day to begin? Or do you feel that separating from electronic devices is naive? Give it a try and see how you feel. See how it works for you or doesn't. And offer the idea to your students.

Chapter 8

On Portals

Expand the Reach of the Classroom

When a teacher commits to reach beyond the classroom, she engages students to seek broader horizons.

We live in a global world. How might we create portals for students to connect to this world? To provide opportunities to reach a larger audience? To become global citizens?

On the surface, if we choose this path, we might be seen as wanting to emulate the celebrity-seeking culture. Already, students are on TikTok, Instagram, and Snapchat. Why encourage them to seek a larger audience? Why not leave such matters to the adult world?

After a long week with her fifth graders, Holly Alan, who often pushed the envelope in her teaching, watched the movie *Julie and Julia*.[1] Julie Powell, who was unemployed at the time, cooked and blogged her way through Julia Child's *Mastering the Art of French Cooking*. Her persistence intrigued a *New York Times* reporter to write a review, which opened a portal into a wider world well beyond Julie's blog circle and led to publishing a book and later a movie.

Having taught fifth grade for nearly ten years, Holly often reflected on her teaching: *When I think about it, my classroom is like every classroom in my school. It is a private world inside the school, itself an inherently closed institution. Despite being publicly funded, my colleagues and I often consider our classrooms as our private domains.*

Holly wondered what her friend and neighbor Nancy Carney, an energetic sixth-grade language arts teacher, thought about the isolated classroom.

"Interesting you should ask," Nancy said. "My colleagues and I have been attempting to connect with one another and to places beyond our school. It's been quite a process. We began this year by having our students write letters and essays to each other in class instead of always writing for 'the teacher.'

We expanded this approach and had students write letters (yes, letters!) to students in other grades and even to students in other schools. What was exciting, their writing improved—and they received interesting responses. Some have formed pen pals, most switching to texting.

"Given our successes, we upped the level, having them write letters and commentaries to newspapers and later to selected blogs. We then connected our teaching to issues that concern the community; we began by focusing on stream pollution. We taught them how to write petitions to local government officials about our findings. This was challenging but was well worth it.

"This led to our using the Internet to connect with a school in Finland. We had our first Skype connection last week in which we discussed what we might achieve together. Luckily, the Finnish kids know English."

After her conversation with Nancy, Holly recalled Julie Powell's movie. Unlike celebrity breakouts that result in fifteen minutes of fame, Julie's came from a strong work ethic. Her blog opened her to a wider network that ultimately came to the attention of the *New York Times*. It's one way the real world works.

Holly realized, both from the movie and from her conversation with Nancy, that she could open ways for her students to reach out sensibly to the larger world. She would teach them how to set a goal and persist to its conclusion. She would help them become proud to share their learning not only with each other and their families but also through portals to other interested parties. In the process, she would nurture the importance of a strong work ethic as Julie had as a cook and blogger.

Perhaps her classroom could create its own blog? That could be a good beginning.

REFLECTION/ACTION

What are your thoughts about having your students reach out into the larger world? What could work? What might not? If you choose to open portals to go beyond your classroom, what would you choose to do? How would you integrate it with the curriculum responsibilities you have?

PART II

Reflections: Pondering Possibilities

Taking time to reflect on practice invites teachers to consider alternative ways to reach today's students.

Choosing to consider the ideas in each of these chapters can lead to improving your teaching. Each taps into your creative self. Each invites you to step outside your practice and consider alternatives. Read each one at a time to consider its wisdom and respond to the Reflection/Action queries and write your first impressions. Give thought as to how these ideas can inform your practice. And share them with colleagues if you are so moved. Who knows what conversations might ensue.

Chapter 9

On Conversation

Invoke Reflective Talking and Listening

> *When teachers enact face-to-face conversations, classrooms have a sense of purpose, thoughtfulness, and adventure.*

Bill Murthy was wondering why his students were not responsive in his class discussions. He often had to move them along, more than he wanted, because he believed they would be better served were he more of an observer. "I want them to become agents in their education. I can't be the one who always feeds them. They need to feed themselves."

"Mr. Murthy's" general demeanor was on the quiet side. He was eager to have his students learn but did not push. He hoped his presence, when calm, thoughtful, and warm, would invite his students into thinking about what they were learning.

One afternoon, in his favorite bookstore, he discovered Margaret Wheatley's, *Turning to One Another: Simple Conversations to Restore Hope to the Future*.[1] After reading it, he decided to introduce Wheatley's framework for conversation to his ninth graders.

We acknowledge one another as equals.
We try to stay curious about each other.
We recognize that we need each other's help to become better listeners.
We slow down so we have time to think and reflect.
We remember that conversation is the natural way we humans think together.
We expect it to be messy at times.[2]

We acknowledge one another as equals. To invoke this principle, Bill emphasized building trust. He wanted to allow for authenticity, honesty, and risk. No student would sit in fear of giving a wrong answer or asking a stupid question.

Minds would become free to explore their own or other's ideas, peers in pursuit of questions, perplexities, and understandings. They would arrive at unexpected destinations. If necessary, he could have them agree to let what was said "stay in Vegas." It would be all good.

Putting chairs in a circle—a new idea for him—would help his students see themselves as equals. By not having to look at the backs of the heads of their peers, they would relate with one another and with him.

We try to stay curious about each other. Bill, having grown up in a gregarious family, has always been curious about people around him. He makes it a point to greet each student as they come into his room, often asking a personal question or making a personal comment.

But he wondered, because his students spend six to seven hours a day alone on their phones, if was hindering their ability to engage in real conversations. Curious about their fixed attention to their phones (he still had a flip phone), he invited them to share their thoughts. The ensuing conversations led him to ask questions, which stimulated their curiosity. He would insert "teaching moments" inside these conversations. Things were warming up, he thought.

We recognize that we need each other's help to become better listeners. Bill was convinced that the hours spent attending to phones curtailed his students' ability to listen to each other. Even though phones were not allowed in his room (except for instruction), students appeared distracted. Some were no doubt anticipating what they would find on social media when getting their phones back. He decided to take time away from the curriculum to focus on listening.

He introduced two exercises. The first was inside-outside circles. He divided the class in half, placing students in two circles facing each other. Then he assigned a topic. The inside person would speak first for a minute; the outside person would have a minute to respond. After each person spoke, Bill rang a bell; the second time he rang it signaled students on the outside to take one step to the left to meet a new partner. The process repeated until the last pair. And the other requirement—important!—students had to look at each other in the eye in the process.

The second exercise was an extension of inside-outside circles using the same procedure. It had specific content, for example, Robert Frost's "The Road Not Taken." After the first person's one-minute comment about the poem, the responder had to repeat what he heard as best as he could. Having to repeat, Bill hoped it would help them to listen more attentively.

He followed up by teaching them how to paraphrase and how to mirror and validate what a person says. He believed validation to be doubly important because it encourages empathy, something he has seen lacking in many of his students.

We slow down so we have time to think and reflect. Every day, Bill does his best to be open as to what happens in his classroom. He stays in the moment, listens without forming thoughts, and slows down whenever he can to counter the busyness of the school day. He resists having anxiety about the future and concerns over which he has no control. He wants his class conversations to invite pondering, choosing, and retaining—for his students and for him.

When on their phones for six to seven hours a day, students process fast-paced information that flows in and out, in and out. No time to stop and invite reflection. He includes pauses during class discussions for that purpose. Sometimes, he would ask them to reflect in writing on what has been said. Giving the brain time to retain would improve long-term memory, necessary for thinking and problem solving. Where else will they have this opportunity?

We remember that conversation is the natural way we humans think together. Throughout human history, the nature of conversation has changed. Early humans employed language by sitting around campfires telling stories; their memories stored knowledge. The introduction of writing allowed for communication without having to memorize. Gutenberg's press enabled printed books that allowed for connection through uninterrupted solitude, the thoughts of the writer communicating to the reader. In the late nineteenth century, the invention of the telephone enabled voice-to-voice connections, sightless conversations but conversations nonetheless.

The Internet and wireless devices have taken the world in a new direction, which often leads to communication without conversation. Social networks dominate. People instantly see what they think they want to know, respond to it, or pass it on—and are likely to forget what they just read. Like skipping stones.

Bill understands that his classroom may be one of the last places where students can be together face-to-face without devices, where they can learn to speak and listen while looking one another in the eye. It's a privilege he cherishes.

As for his part in the conversation process, he visualizes a thread that passes through each person who speaks—and, as he observes the flow, he curtails the number of times the thread of conversation passes through him. He wants his students to depend on one another.

We expect it to be messy at times. When Bill let go of trying to stay in control, surprises emerged, insights abounded, and joy surfaced. Messiness invited originality, while routines stifled creativity. His best conversations with students happened when they took on lives of their own.

Like all good teachers, Bill makes plans. Sometimes his students subvert them; they move off topic and occasionally succeed. Most of the time he finds a way to stay in the vicinity of his intentions but recognizes that some of his best lessons come from exciting detours. Conversations spawn unforeseen insights never before imagined. Insights from his students. Insights from him.

Bill decided to introduce Wheatley's six principles one at a time. Processing each of them would enable students to grasp them thoroughly. Following Wheatley's advice, he stayed curious, listened openly, slowed down to reflect, let conversations happen, and allowed for messiness. He was pleased with how well his students responded.

REFLECTION/ACTION

How do you respond to Wheatley's framework for conversations? How might you incorporate each of them into your classroom? Conversations level the playing field. In partnership, teacher and students think, process, ask questions, give opinions, and express feelings, each person able to choose what to say and believe. It's a two-way process that offers choices to students—and teacher.

Chapter 10

On Macro Keys

Apply Technology to Improve Writing

> *A teacher's decision to use technology to engage with his students' writing assured that they rewrote their drafts.*

In 1984, Chet Kozjanski was in his tenth year of teaching eighth grade. He loved his job; eighth grade was his nirvana. Their adolescent minds at moments teetered from the brilliant to the despondent, from exhilaration to despair. Listening to them, whether in class conversations or through their writing, was the reason he looked forward to Mondays.

He had to rely on his hard-to-read handwriting to prepare lesson plans, draft his handouts, and to write tests (his school had a secretary who typed them on dittos). It was a time-consuming process.

In May of that year, Chet got his first Macintosh. As soon as it arrived, he opened its Picasso box and slowly lifted out the 128K state-of-the-art, beige-colored computer, keyboard, and mouse. From a second box, he took out an ImageWriter printer, a hard drive, and a small box of three-and-one-half-inch floppy disks. He plugged in the Macintosh and turned it on. A dual-face, line-drawn image materialized in the middle of the nine-inch monochromic display screen. He could hardly contain himself!

After referring to the manual for setup, he put it aside. He discovered how easily he could navigate the menu. Before long he became one with his beloved Macintosh. The manual collected dust.

Chet was thrilled that he could now easily read and edit his writing. Finally, his students will actually be able to read it! He had given up using a typewriter, as he erased as much as he typed. Tapping with two fingers on his keyboard, he found a new sense of freedom. He did not have to ask the faculty secretary to struggle to interpret his handwriting when she typed his tests. He saw himself as his own Gutenberg, a one-man publishing house.

Fifteen years later, Chet took a job as an eighth-grade teacher at a different school. This one had a computer lab, where students could write papers. No need for handwritten drafts. Chet liked this approach more than some of his colleagues, who insisted that students write their drafts in longhand.

When his students composed their papers in the computer lab, he discovered that many of them ignored his suggestions for revising. They simply reprinted their first drafts; the papers looked good typed, so why not just reprint them? It did not take Chet long to figure out what they were doing. He really couldn't blame them. Such "perfect-looking" papers.

But he believed writing was about rethinking, revising, rewriting. About having to respond to feedback, which was his responsibility. He arranged for his students not to print out their first drafts but to drop them into a class folder on the computer. Chet then would access their papers on his computer and offer critique and comments.

It would take time to process each student's draft—drafts from the five folders, one for each class! He developed the idea of using the macro-keys option with shortcut keys. He preprogrammed words or phrases on the keys to insert as comments into their drafts. He used a bold 14-point Helvetica font in stark contrast to the Times 12-point he required from his students.

His macros included prompts indicating spelling and grammar errors, suggestions to restructure sentences, make organizational changes, and revise content. He also inserted question marks and brackets in Helvetica around poorly written sentences and paragraphs to indicate revision. Students had to purge his notations and (hopefully) revise and reformat their papers and resubmit them into the computer folder.

The result, students did make revisions. And they appreciated not having to take time to print out hard copies—and perhaps the best benefit, not having to decipher Mr. Kozjanski's poorly handwritten comments. Their writing became more seamless. And the school saved lots of paper! This process meant more thinking and work for them—and for Mr. Kozjanski—but resulted in better papers.

Chet's decision demonstrates the importance of teachers staying abreast of the culture in which their students reside. Had he insisted on handwritten drafts, for example, he would have been imposing a Luddite culture; they would not have been prepared to live and work inside the world of ubiquitous word processing. Had he asked, they would have done handwritten drafts.

Years later, Chet discovered Google Docs and had an epiphany. Why not have students use Google Docs to prepare cooperative papers? He was sure they would learn from each other and perhaps gain good ideas about their writing. On "important" papers, he would have them interact only with him. He would make on-the-spot comments to encourage rethinking and rewriting.

Writing remains fundamental to education. People learn by writing and rewriting and rewriting. Regardless of which technology they choose, the writing depends upon writers doing the work. Incorporating the power of macros in the mid-1990s allowed Chet to help students make a smooth transition, taking advantage of the world of word processing. Many students thanked him for his efforts. They were becoming better writers.

Since the mid-2000s, Chet has been using Google Docs to open dialogues between him and his young writers. He is discovering ways to help his students become better thinkers and writers. And he has become a better teacher—and a better writer.

With the arrival of GPT-4, Chet wonders whether he would be able to tackle its challenges. He is close to retirement.

REFLECTION/ACTION

Do you consider ways to become a better teacher? How well do you take advantage of new technologies? Are you able to sort out how to separate "good" technology from the "bad" for your classroom? Do you listen to how your students respond? Allowing yourself time to reflect on these and other questions can bring you to new places, new actions that improve learning for you and your students.

Chapter 11

On Metaphor

Put Student Learning First

A teacher's decision to "drive" a metro minibus rather than a yellow school bus signifies her commitment to pay attention to her students' learning.

When Martha Uzersky was thinking about becoming a teacher, she believed her curiosity would be a catalyst for her students. In college, she was an exuberant history major known as a philosophical maverick who frequently connected seemingly unrelated ideas into a coherent whole.

In her tenth year teaching ninth-grade social studies, she was wrestling with a conundrum: how to bring knowledge into her classroom and at the same time have students energetically respond. She wanted to find a doorway to have shared learning with them. They liked her quirky delivery, her wandering through the aisles adding humor to the mix. But she wanted to be able to draw more from them.

One evening, after she and her students had spent the previous two weeks analyzing Confucian analects, sayings, she realized she was on to something. The discussions were often intense, even fierce, students trying to convince one another about their takes on Confucius's filial piety, or why a child should or should not "remonstrate" his father. On a whim, instead of giving a test she decided to ask them to write their own analects. They were remarkable, so much so she decided to "publish" them into a booklet to give to them.

Six examples (she gave students "Chinese" names):

- Trev-Mar said to Confucius while driving him past a village, "The man who believes all that he hears without question is the inferior man."
- Cait-lin, a whimsical disciple of Confucius who loved to run in the woods, quipped, "In a race it is more fun to beat the boys than to draw hearts around their names."

- Josh-lu, devoted disciple of Confucius, asked, "Which is more important, self or others?" Confucius replied, "Without self, there are no others, and without others, there is no self."
- As Sean-Ginn, a devoted disciple of Confucius wrote, "Listen to those who talk to you and you in turn will be heard."
- In reflecting the wisdom of Confucius, Dor-si, a devoted and reverent follower, said, "Kindness is like a stream of water. It makes rough tough rocks smooth." Confucius rode on with a broad smile on his face.

That evening, Martha wrote in her journal:

I've been paying attention to my students' learning for years now. Teaching, as I envision it now, is about making a choice whether to drive a yellow school bus or a metro minibus. If I persist in delivery—to cover "required" material—I will be choosing to drive a yellow school bus with students sitting in pairs on both sides of the aisle. I check to see if everyone is in their seat. When I start "driving," I turn on the PA. I point out "sites" along a pre-marked path to fulfill my "lesson" plan, arriving at each site on time. Most days, my yellow bus reaches its intended destination. On the days it doesn't, I make it up the next day.

But, if I were to decide to engage students—to put learning first—I will be choosing to drive a metro minibus with informal-style seating. As students enter, I greet them by name. They sit face to face. I drive the bus on a road serving as our guide, our intention, but in no way is our route foreordained. As forks and sidetracks appear, I sometimes take one. I pay attention to my students' observations.

I turn the bus to the right, to the left, or continue straight on. I stop to allow my students to savor where we are. I may retrace our path so they might better understand where we have been. I bring the bus to a meaningful destination, not always to the one intended.

I choose to drive the minibus. My classroom belongs to me and to my students. If I decide to have them only listen to me, together plowing through the "expected" plan as a driver of the yellow school bus, I would be denying their presence. I might think that I am "doing good," but I'd have no idea what they are learning. They might be daydreaming and missing a whole section on what I am talking about; getting back on track becomes nearly impossible.

I like the metro minibus metaphor. I intend to share it with my department colleagues, perhaps at a less formal meeting time where we have time for an extended conversation; it could be somewhat contentious but could lead to new understandings. I am thinking especially about my veteran colleagues who feel their responsibility is to delivery knowledge on schedule to students.

Closing her journal, she said to herself, "We live in interesting times."

Martha believes teachers should choose to be the teachers they want to be. In the privacy of their classrooms, they can choose to engage in conversations and invoke partnerships with their students' thinking. She wonders how many of her colleagues agree with her.

A few evenings later, Martha wrote in her journal about what practices she intended to be sure not to do:

> No longer will I insert rote knowledge and skills into the minds of unsuspecting students. No longer will I insist that they copy down whatever I say just because I say it.
>
> No longer will I race through material, give quizzes and a unit test, and then move directly to the next unit when some students have not learned the current material.
>
> No longer will I have to pretend that all students come to my classes well prepared.
>
> And [she added], I will arrange desks so students can look at each other.

Martha was grateful to have committed to her students' learning. However, some of her department colleagues were annoyed with her, because she resisted sticking with the preplanned curriculum. And some questioned why she does not come to the faculty room during her planning period. What she doesn't tell them is that she doesn't want to listen to complaints about the administration, other teachers, and students.

She detests the department's expectation to set aside time for test preparation; it takes time away from her teaching. If she teaches literacy skills thoroughly and consistently—to read critically, to think and write with rigor, and to develop argumentative skills—students will succeed on tests. Convincing her colleagues will be hard.

As a twenty-first-century teacher, Martha focuses on communication skills, critical thinking, performance abilities, and depth of knowledge and understanding. She partners with students in assessing their learning. And she is sure that when she talks less and listens more, they will become more engaged in conversations.

Once Martha found the chutzpah to choose to drive the metro minibus, she took a less-traveled road to serve her students well. Were she to deliver curricula at a set pace, she would remain on the yellow school bus condoning a culture of delivering curricula at a specified pace. "Not for me," she said to herself. "And not for my students. I want them to develop self-knowledge and be free to make choices. Otherwise, they will not be educated."

REFLECTION/ACTION

How do you respond to Martha Uzersky's arguments in support of driving the minibus instead of the yellow school bus? Does the metaphor make sense? If so, which bus do you see yourself on? Does her reflection invite you to try practices that might help you better connect with the gifts and strengths of your students? And to yours?

Chapter 12

On the Four Agreements

Find Your Center

Wisdom from the ancients and mystics invites us to find solace and center ourselves in our work. The Four Agreements provide one such path.

Teachers work inside complex environments. Chaos overwhelms, some days more than others. To find solace, some choose to seek relief from a partner, a friend, or a colleague. Others choose to sit quietly after school in their classroom, take a walk by the ocean or on a mountain path, sit in meditation, read poetry, or veg out with a movie.

Once in a while, insights arrive over the transom. Jamie Peters, a middle school social studies teacher known for his quiet compassion, was in his favorite bookstore when Don Miguel Ruiz's *The Four Agreements* practically fell off a shelf into his hands. He often perused the store's spiritual bookshelves to find wisdom to help him be more patient with his eighth graders—and himself.

For nearly ten years, he had been searching for meaning behind the obvious in his teaching. In grade-level meetings, he often came back to his major concern: what really matters in teaching. For example, when reintroducing his students to Confucius, Lao Tzu, and the Buddha, he rediscovered his love for ancient philosophers. He found himself learning alongside his students.

The Four Agreements is a small book, less than 140 pages in a five-by-seven-inch, large-print format. Its author, Don Miguel Ruiz, a Mexican Toltec master, offers "a personal guide to freedom."[1] A tall order from such a small venue, Jamie thought. Yet, he needed several readings to absorb the meaning of each agreement:

1. Be impeccable with your word.
2. Don't take anything personally.

3. Don't make assumptions.
4. Always do your best.

Be impeccable with your word. Jamie understood that the first Agreement means to speak with integrity, not to gossip about others *or* to speak against ourselves. It begins with our impeccable thinking, our thought words and internal conversations. From these come spoken words, to use their power in the direction of truth and love. For Jamie, his words become seeds for his students and for himself.

Jamie believes the same holds true for listening. When he hears others speak about him, he does not believe what is not true; internalizing untruths is harmful. The giver of gossip does not succeed unless the receiver accepts it. He sees it in today's culture where false information purveyors find believers.

"When you are impeccable," Ruiz writes, "you take responsibility for your actions, but you do not judge or blame yourself."[2] Jamie takes responsibility for his actions, but he struggles with self-judgment. Given that teachers are frequently blamed for society's failures, no wonder he and many of his colleagues are sensitive to criticism.

Jamie wonders: *Am I impeccable when I choose not to say what I think? Am I being impeccable with my thoughts?*

Don't take anything personally. In the second agreement, Ruiz offers a way out from under the influence of others—a way to become true to ourselves. When we take things personally, we agree with what people say about us, becoming a matter of "personal importance," where everything is "about me." We believe we are responsible for everything. Ultimately, Ruiz says—and here he surprises Jamie—taking everything personally is a matter of maximum selfishness.[3]

Ruiz points out that when we agree with opinions that hurt us, we allow them to become poison. Our goal is to live in our own movie (as others live in theirs)—accept ourselves, and live with love and without fear. "When we are immune to the opinions and actions of others, we won't be the victim of needless suffering."[4]

Ultimately, not taking anything personally gives Jamie a personal freedom (gaining personal freedom, the underlying message of *The Four Agreements*). And Jamie understands when he hears a comment directed to him, that person is also talking about himself. The same is true when he says something to another.

Don't make assumptions. "One thing, Mr. Peters, that bothered me when I was in your eighth-grade class, now nearly ten years ago," Regan told him, "you seemed to decide early on which of us was smart and which were not—and you never changed your mind!"

Regan's insight was an epiphany for Jamie. From that moment, he would be even more conscious of each of his students' potential. He would try to see them as they were at that moment, not as who he thought they were. He reminded himself that he needed to do this every day.

Ruiz writes, "We have a tendency to make assumptions about everything. The problem with making assumptions is that we *believe* that they are the truth."[5] When Jamie notes that a colleague makes an assumption about him, he calmly ignores the comment or chooses to ask clarifying questions. He is invoking a piece of the personal freedom that Ruiz wants for him and everyone.

In terms of relationships, Ruiz writes, "Real love is accepting other people the way they are without trying to change them. If we try to change them, it means we don't really like them."[6] Strong words for a teacher to hear. Jamie wonders: *How can my teaching be an act of love, if my aim is in part to change some students?*

Ruiz offers a way out: "Find the courage to ask questions and express what you really want. Communicate with others as clearly as you can to avoid misunderstandings, sadness, and drama."[7] Jamie decided to open his classes to having more conversations to keep him close to seeing his students as they are.

Always do your best. To do our best is a fluid process; we must commit to it every minute. We do not judge ourselves. As *The Bhagavad-Gita* states, we should not become attached to our results.

Of all the Agreements, Jamie found the fourth the most straightforward. Ruiz cautions to be vigilant, because we can easily fail when we decide to take shortcuts, cut corners, make wrong turns, and act slothful.

He recalled as a young teacher aiming to earn a professional contract, he was driven to do his best to impress students, colleagues, and supervisors. Secure with tenure, he has made a conscious effort to do his best but not to impress anyone else. Doing his best is his obligation to his students and school community—and to himself.

Toward the end of the book, Ruiz invites readers to make another Agreement, "I choose to honor the Four Agreements."[8] Knowing that we are doing our best allows us to pursue this path without self-judgment.

As a Toltec, Ruiz lives with no leaders and no followers "where you have your own truth and live your truth."[9] To find personal freedom is a choice. It's up to us. And how we live with ourselves is how we treat others.

Jamie realizes in choosing to follow the Four Agreements, he will have to challenge his department's protocols, including its emphasis on test prep and testing, on department teachers having to teach the same material in the same time frame, and on sticking close to the textbook.

By sharing his choice to seek personal freedom through his actions, Jamie lets his students know they can seek theirs. He does his best to be impeccable with his word, not react personally, avoid making assumptions, and always doing his best. When a student lies, Jamie speaks truth. When a student swears, Jamie holds his tongue. When a child hates, Jamie loves. And when a child fails to try, Jamie encourages. He is grateful for the gift of *The Four Agreements*.

REFLECTION/ACTION

Reflect on each of the Four Agreements for yourself; there's much to absorb. Choose how to respond to each one. Take your time. Consider how each of these Agreements could impact your teaching. How could you introduce them to your students? If inclined, read Ruiz's *The Four Agreements* to dwell further into his thinking.[10]

PART III

Insights: The Wisdom of Contemplating Ideas

*Beyond the paradigm of traditional teaching practices reside
ideas to awaken new methods and approaches.*

Ideas for better teaching abound. Each of these chapters, again to be read one at a time, invites you to consider insights from a wide range of sources. Learn from the strength of a bystander and from a painter who recognizes that everything has its own speed, discover the insufficiency of PowerPoint, and be surprised by Frank's choice to sit alone.

Take time to consider each of these chapters one at a time and respond to each Reflection/Action section, taking a few minutes to write your first thoughts. Again, as with all the chapters in this book, share with colleagues whom you think would respond to these insights.

Chapter 13

On the Bystander
Choose Non-action

> *In responding to frenetic moments, an older man's non-action reveals the strength of standing still.*

Bystanders wait.

In a world seeking fifteen minutes of fame, a bystander's non-action may appear as nonsense. In our need to solve a problem, we may prefer to be proactive. If we choose to sit and contemplate, we might feel we will miss opportunities—or perceived opportunities.

When we lose our keys, we rush around and try to find them rather than sit still and let our mind recall where they are. We ride the merry-go-round in anticipation of reaching the gold ring, rather than taking pleasure in riding the merry-go-round to ride the merry-go-round.[1]

Elissa Ely reminds us of the bystander. In her brief essay, she describes a reality cooking show in which chefs compete in teams. During the relay segment, each chef was allowed ten minutes to work the recipe before the next chef (who was blindfolded) had to figure out what to do. Their energy was frenetic, except for one older man who appeared immobile in front of his frying pan.

> Gladiators ran past while he stood in his apron. After about a minute of stillness, his face started to glow with a look of comprehension. He understood what he needed to do. Newton's apple had fallen, and he was in position to receive it. Now, he was ready to cook it.[2]

How often during a lesson have you chosen non-action? Recognizing simply to stop to contemplate rather than hurry on to the next thing. Asking for or allowing time for non-action. To be present. In Ely's metaphor, to be open to "when and where the apple will drop."

Meditation reminds you to take time to simply be. To wait, become receptive, spontaneous, and open. See what you need and allow it to come to you. You decide to emulate the "Taoist," Winnie the Pooh, and his uncanny ability to be in accord with the way things are—*wu wei*, do without doing—like water that flows unimpeded on a path of least resistance.[3]

Sometimes you find yourself in a flurry. Everything comes at you all at once. Everyone around you acts like Ely's gladiator chefs. You want to find a way out before you are consumed. You sense you have no control.

In such moments, you would do well to invoke firefighter Norman McLean's decision to stand still in the face of an oncoming raging forest fire. Instead of seeking a way to flee, McLean started to burn the grass around him so as to deny the fire fuel. Thirteen of his men thought he was crazy and fled on a path that appeared open to cliffs nearby. They all died, but McLean and one other survived.[4]

In your classroom, you can choose not to flee when students press you, when events take over. You assess what's happening. You allow others to see where they are and what they are doing. When lost, you trust the trees in the forest to know where you are.[5] You allow time for the pressing event to retreat. You deprive it of its fuel, a Norman McLean reprieve, to give students time to choose to come back to you.

Ely's older man won the competition, much to the envy of the other frenetic chefs. She writes, "Speed under stress is considered a form of mastery, but slowing down—resisting instinct, drive, and all biology—is gladiatorial." When bewildering concerns toss you about, you do not need to breed that confusion into students.

As a teacher, you can trust deep understanding and choose to curtail this spiraling downward and, instead, open students to the joys of learning. Learning that drops in. Learning from each other. From the world. From inside. From non-action.

REFLECTION/ACTION

When the frenetic fray of rushed school life impedes, how will you find ways to create moments to step back? In anticipation, invite your students to engage in reflective conversations and to express their thoughts and feelings. Gather alongside them as a bystander pausing to let learning in, together becoming like the older man who stood calm in the storm.

Chapter 14

On Lesson Plans

Focus on Learning

When teachers remain flexible with their plans, they emphasize what students are learning.

Lesson plans. Sometimes it seems teaching is all about lesson plans. Some departments require them to be submitted a week ahead of time; others even further ahead. Lesson plans ensure that teachers keep pace with the curriculum. In some schools, departments decide on their curriculum, but in many schools the sequence of textbook chapters define it. Having lesson plans in place assumes the sequence will be carried out.

The lesson-plan mindset is about control. If a department insists on submitting plans for the week, it is indicating for teachers to stay in line. The department can then report to the administration that everyone is fulfilling expectations, that things are "moving along" as they should. But the missing element in this paradigm is the students. What is happening in their minds? What are they taking away each day? What will they remember? How well will they do on the exam?

Many teachers expect to take students through a preplanned journey and get through the material. They prepare careful outlines, put key terms on the whiteboard, and sometimes provide handouts in class or on a website.

Insisting on this approach misses the mark. Lecture-type lessons may be fine in university, but they do not belong in school classrooms. Learning in class must be the focus, not taking notes to process later. Learning requires interacting with students, listening to them, explaining, repeating. It means paying attention to each one and knowing how well they are learning, and more important, what they are understanding.[1]

It is unfair to think of students as receptacles, as takers-in of what a teacher delivers and expects them to learn. On the other hand, if a teacher is to educate, to "lead out"—*educere* from Latin—he needs to let his students know where he's headed. And if he is wise, he will include them in setting the path.

How can departments remedy this outmoded form of lesson planning? What can they do to activate teacher-student learning in the classroom? Begin with a different assumption: it is not about lesson plans but about what students will learn. To make this possible, conversations are necessary in the classroom, in department, and in faculty meetings. And conversations take time. To expect each child to learn at the pace of a teacher's plan is unrealistic and always has been. Teachers know after a few weeks which students are going to "get it," which ones will need more time, and which are likely not to "get it."

An essential component in a different planning paradigm makes room for student input, reflections, ruminations. Prepare big ideas, but allow for responses in determining the outcome; you may get to only part of your intentions, but you can circle back. You live in a world that has more information than anyone can manage. People try to keep up with all that surrounds them, flipping through their devices, and find themselves in an endless scramble. Amid the chaos, the classroom can be a special place, a place for centering. Students can come to know who they are, not in response to what comes their way, but in who they see themselves to be.

Students reside at the center of your classroom. Pay attention to their paying attention. Arrange your room to fit the needs of the moment. For example, make a circle for discussion so students can look each other in the eye. Adjust assessments to fit the needs of the subject at hand.

In the conversation classroom, you form a partnership with your students to search for what matters, what will propel them to become lifelong learners. Knowledge is not enough; understanding is essential. Teaching is not telling; it is making learning happen. Asking students to take in information for a class period and expecting it to be learned at home deprives them of learning alongside you. Instead, you want them to self-develop and be free to make choices.

The focus of good lesson planning ensures that learning is accessible to all students. It is especially important when presenting information not to deliver non-stop lectures without feedback, certain to leave many students behind.

Confronting the embedded tradition of lesson planning will take persistence. To invite students' thinking to become central to the direction of the class will be a paradigm shift. Incorporating conversation to learn what students are thinking and questioning makes delivery secondary. Conversations invite young minds to contribute as well as to listen to the teacher and to each other. The amount of knowledge "covered" may be less, but the learning will be more.

REFLECTION/ACTION

Lesson plans have been the heart of teaching. In some departments, they can become straitjackets, forcing you to strictly follow a plan with no room for movement and no opportunity to take into account what happens to your students. Consider rethinking their place in your teaching if need be, and consider your students and what you want them to learn. As you engage in a lesson, let go when it veers and see where you and your students arrive. Imagine, too, your students leaving class taking their learning with them rather than having to try to remember "the lesson" at home.

Chapter 15

On Everything Has Its Own Speed
Don't Kill the Butterfly

> *Life in the rush-rush, digitally driven world calls for educators to slow to the speed of things as they are.*

"You can't go faster than the paint," a wise Brazilian house painter told me when he painted my ceiling. Such wisdom lurks everywhere. Life's complications in this digital world pushes people to act rashly, to jump to solutions but not arrive. The Brazilian's wise words give pause. Everything has its own speed.

In the classroom, you feel captured by pressures to get to the end of a lesson before the bell. Unsuspected intrusions show up: a tussle between students breaks out, the fire alarm sounds, an angry parent bursts into the room, a lawnmower roars beneath the window, the principal calls over the intercom—and calls again five minutes later asking for reports due yesterday. To not "go faster than the paint" can be hard, very hard.

Consider the words of Nikos Kazantzakis:

> I remember one morning when I discovered a cocoon in the bark of a tree, just as a butterfly was making a hole in its case and preparing to come out. I waited a while, but it was too long appearing and I was impatient. I bent over it and breathed on it to warm it. I warmed it as quickly as I could and the miracle began to happen right before my eyes, faster than life. The case opened, the butterfly started slowly crawling out and I shall never forget my horror when I saw how its wings were folded back and crumpled; the wretched butterfly tried with its whole trembling body to unfold them. Bending over it, I tried to help with my breath. In vain.
>
> It needed to be hatched out patiently and the unfolding of the wings should be a gradual process in the sun. Now it was too late. My breath had forced the butterfly to appear, all crumpled, before its time. It struggled desperately and, a few seconds later, died in the palm of my hand.

> That little body is, I do believe, the greatest weight I have on my conscience. For I realize today that it is a mortal sin to violate the great laws of nature. We should not hurry, we should not be impatient, but we should obey the eternal rhythm.[1]

Kazantzakis implores us to "obey the eternal rhythm," to care for and respect the needs of others, to listen before asking, wait before coaxing, hesitate before prodding. Again, everything at its own speed, every person at his own speed.

When tempted to rush to complete a task, remember that students are a collection of individuals. Pay close attention to those who are not "getting it." Invite others who do to help bring their classmates along. Rushing through to complete may satisfy supervisors—but it may fail students.

Pay close attention to each student's insights. After some months, a boy still reads more slowly than his classmates; he says he reads that way because he wants to remember everything while pondering questions in his mind. Others in the class reveal their own particularities; a girl prefers to read lying down on the carpet, another works better with a partner, and a few may complain about having to work in a cluster. Paying attention reveals the classroom as a collection of individuals working "at their own speed," in their own way.

Thich Nhat Hanh's wisdom about "washing the dishes to wash the dishes"[2] reinforces paying attention. To wash the dishes means to wash the dishes, not to get them clean, not to watch TV after but to wash the dishes. And when rushing, water splashes all over the counter, sometimes a plate breaks, and frustration arises. But staying in the moment, the dishes get done at the speed of the soap and water.

Pay attention to your practice. Balance the urge to finish the lesson with paying attention to student receptivity; bring ideas into harmony. Good teaching depends upon teachers listening. When forgetting, come back to the moment. Choose not to act "faster than life." Do not kill the butterfly.

Jennifer L. Roberts gives an assignment to her art history students: to spend *three full hours* viewing a painting, noting their observations while all the time staying disconnected from electronic devices. This process is about, in Robert's words, "deceleration, patience, and immersive attention" to counter external pressures "social and technological . . . pushing students in the other direction, toward immediacy, rapidity, and spontaneity."[3]

Despite not having the option to invoke Roberts's three-hour assignment, you can learn about the power of taking time to contemplate. Invite your students to immerse themselves in an idea, an image, a story. Inserting such times of deceleration reaps unforeseen benefits. Being contemplative brings solace, something sorely lacking in the rush of today's digitally driven culture.

Again, in Kazantzakis's words, do not act "faster than life . . . and violate the great laws of nature"—and do not kill the butterfly.

REFLECTION/ACTION

What was your reaction when you first read "you can't go faster than the paint"? To "everything has its own speed"? To "obey the eternal rhythm" and not to kill the butterfly? And to Jennifer Roberts's assignment to spend three hours in front of a painting? What do these have to say about your teaching? Is it possible for you to find such spaces in your classroom, or are you under pressure to complete expected assignments? If you want to commit to learning alongside your students—to let each cocoon unfold naturally—are you willing to go out on a limb if you feel you have to and allow that to happen?

Chapter 16

On PowerPoint

See the Emperor Not Wearing Any Clothes

> *When teachers pay attention to PowerPoint's template format, they recognize its failure to communicate.*

In April 1987, Microsoft introduced PowerPoint for Macintosh computers. PowerPoint quickly became ubiquitous slide-ware, the main format for projecting and delivering information to groups in schools, colleges, and business groups throughout the world. Edward Tufte estimated that 10^{10} to 10^{11} PowerPoint slides are made each year.[1] Ubiquitous totally.

What are its implications for classrooms? When a teacher chooses to use PowerPoint's prepared templates, she becomes a deliverer and her students recipients. Both teacher and students are captive to its appeal. But students become confused when the teachers' words differ from words on the screen.

Captive may be an exaggeration, but upon further examination, perhaps not. Tufte's *The Cognitive Style of PowerPoint* offers a valuable critique. In thirty-two cogent pages, he steps back to examine the implications of PowerPoint, which unlike printed handouts:

- makes for low-resolution slides, at most about forty words on each;
- dumbs down content to fit its limited template formats;
- uses mindless, unrelated bullets;
- fails to provide narrative;
- and all in "an attitude of commercialism that turns everything into a sales pitch."[2]

Tufte provides clear examples: how slides contributed to the Columbia space shuttle disaster; how Peter Novig's supercilious slides of the Gettysburg

Address diminish its impact; and how medical slides, despite their intention, fail to show cancer survival rates. In these and other examples Tufte makes clear that PowerPoint fails to deliver what it promises.

Steve Jobs loathed PowerPoint. When he returned to Apple in 1997, he demanded that product review teams not use it. He later recalled,

> I hate the way people use slide presentations instead of thinking. . . . People would confront problems by creating a presentation. I wanted them to engage, to hash things out at the tables, rather than show a bunch of slides. People who know what they're talking about don't need PowerPoint.[3]

Yet, there are exceptions. Hans Rosling's TED talks demonstrate how PowerPoint at another level enhances thinking and understanding. In his powerful talks on insights into poverty, Rosling, avoiding its prepared templates, created slides in which colored bubbles representing countries move up in wealth, changing in size through time. It is these images and others, which are riveting in support of his words. No templates, no random bullets, no pretty borders. His presentation and animated voice enrapture his audiences.[4]

Without PowerPoint, everyone becomes the center of attention. They observe, listen, and learn from one another. A collective wisdom emerges. They avoid in Tufte's words "playing around with Phluff [his term for PowerPoint content]. Rather than providing information, PowerPoint allows speakers to pretend that they are giving a real talk, and audience to pretend they are listening."[5]

By choosing not to use PowerPoint's slide-ware, teachers avoid a similar predicament that Soviet students in the mid-1980s understood: "Our teachers pretend to teach and we pretend to learn." It was their version of the common Soviet adage: "We pretend to work and they pretend to pay us."

Given the vast number of PowerPoint slides made each year, perhaps massive pretending is happening—and hardly anyone recognizes it!

REFECTION/ACTION

Do you use PowerPoint? Have you thought about its implications? How do you respond to Edward Tufte's critique? To Steve Jobs's reaction? Google Hans Rosling at Ted.com and observe his approach to PowerPoint. Whenever you choose to share information with your students, particularly if using PowerPoint templates, consider carefully how you do it. It's about what they learn, not about what you put on a screen.

Chapter 17

On Symphony
Teach to the Whole Child

One note of a symphony hints at its potential, but all the notes bring it to life—the same holds true for the classroom.

Federal requirements, state mandates, local board demands, and curriculum directives exert excessive pressures on classroom teachers. If all these agencies had their way, teachers would become conduits. But teachers want to provide young people tools for their future, to show them care, to help them to become fulfilled adults and serve their communities. Anything less, and they would be abrogating their responsibility to society.

Today's school landscape offers little room for truly being a teacher. By spending the day telling students what someone else deems important, they would become purveyors, not teachers. They would be performing an expectation that students will regurgitate as best they can on quizzes and tests. Those days should have been numbered a long time ago, but they persist.

Delivering is indoctrination. Students become slates to be written on, not encouraged to have agency, and not allowed to contribute. Their role would be passive: to sit and take in. This process occurred in its extreme in the former Soviet Union. Pedagogy meant students were assigned lessons in texts published by the Party. They were expected to stand to answer questions by repeating the text, then sit down and fold their arms. The same for the next question and the next. No time to discuss. No time to deliberate. The collective took in and spit out the same information.

So, what should you be doing? What would make sense? How do you avoid delivering mandates? First, you remind yourself that you are not a purveyor. Alone in your room, you can subvert. You form partnerships with your students in conversations, putting you and them on a level playing field. You invite thinking, welcoming their thoughts. Learning happens in those moments. What is the use of telling students stuff and expecting them to learn it at home, then come back the next day telling you what they learned (or not)? And you may hesitate to burden them with homework, understanding that it combines with assignments from other classes. And with their day compounded by after-school activities, social media, TikTok, Instagram . . . think about that.

What can you do to make good with students? If your practice reflects the delivery paradigm, begin to move away from it by accepting author Philip Pullman's appeal to act "as if the universe were listening and responding . . . act as if we were going to win."[1] Pullman is reacting to what he calls theocracies that "demonstrate the tendency of human beings to gather power to themselves in the name of something that may not be questioned." School officials can appear inerrant about what they believe you should be doing, having no consideration about what you think.

Pullman argues, "But that doesn't mean we should give up and surrender . . . I think we should act *as if*. I think we should read books, and tell children's stories, and take them to the theatre, and learn poems, and play music, as if it would make a difference." Classrooms need to be places to inspire, to bring students into thinking, aspiring, caring. Standing up front talking and talking does not do it.

When you choose to take an as-if stance, you avoid administering a one-size-fits-all curriculum. You infuse lessons with all the senses, "as if it would make a difference." You act in harmony with the universe. You believe you will win. Anything less and you will be cheating your students—and yourself.

When you choose to act in harmony with the universe, you understand students as having *differentiation*, *communion*, and *autopoiesis*: each child complex and *different*; each with the capacity to connect and *communicate*; and each *self-generating* as discoverer, creator, inventor, and designer.[2] When you recognize this harmony, you will be teaching to the whole symphony.

Schools that focus on test prep, insist on coverage of material, and give high grades to please parents and build the school's reputation will, in effect, be teaching to one note instead of the full symphony. When students graduate, their résumés may look good, but they will not know the potential of their whole selves. They will not be "educated."

No one can become whole without practice at being whole. Delivering a narrow education produces narrow results. If the intention is to develop full human beings, the choice is obvious between repetitive drill-and-kill exercises or invoking classroom conversations.

One more perspective: Christopher McDougall's intriguing book *Born to Run* recounts his fascinating tale of the world's greatest ultra-marathon runners, the Tarahumara Indians of Mexico's Copper Canyon.[3] These ultra-marathoners have made the choice to live whole-symphony lives focused on their love of running. They do not participate in races for recognition and rewards. They do not wear expensive shoes that hurt the feet. They choose not to engage in repetitive rituals for training.

Instead, they learn to run by kicking a wooden ball down rugged paths barefoot as they jump over rocks, roots, and water. The whole symphony of their bodies and minds engaged—and they do it for sheer pleasure. How remarkable would it be if schools were to choose to emulate the Tarahumara's physical intelligence and playful sense of humor. What remarkable symphonies in classrooms would emerge!

Perhaps hanging the photograph from the Apollo 17 spacecraft of blue Earth from space, what Carl Sagan called the "pale blue dot,"[4] would remind your students to seek the full symphony-of-life paradigm. Or perhaps even better, post an image from the James Webb telescope.

REFLECTION/ACTION

Are you encumbered by outside expectations? Do others determine how you are in the classroom? Are you stuck in your "one-note" subject, seeing your students as having to meet it? Or do you remember that you are there to teach students as whole persons? Do you remember that you are there for them to share a love of learning, a love of life? What will you do to ensure that—and that your students know that?

Chapter 18

On Being at the Center

Discover the Internet as a Metaphor for the Universe

> *When teachers recognize the Internet as an expression of the universe, it lets them know that they reside at the center.*

"Where is your classroom?" a colleague asks. You might well answer, as I did in my first year, "My room is number twenty-two on the second floor, diagonally across from the front office." You could also say your classroom is in your community, in your county, your state, nation, hemisphere, the world. And with the recent space explorations through the wondrous eyes of the Hubble telescope and the sophisticated James Webb, you could say that your classroom is in the universe. A small speck, yes, but an important one.

By the end of the twentieth century, the Internet had formed a global community. Any person of any age, race, ethnic group, status, wealth could participate. Africans, Asians, Europeans, and North and South Americans. Young children, teenagers, parents, executives, artists, seniors, et al. No credentials necessary. No one in charge. The Internet had no boss.

Any site is still a click or two away. Sequencing is personal. Hyperlinks create unique pathways. Like the brain's synapses, the Internet leaps almost at will, often taking the user to unimagined places that are full of possibilities—and, unfortunately, places empty with improbabilities. Instant messaging, multitudinous apps, shared-screen interactivity. Given the paradigm of the-whole-is-larger-than-the-sum-of-its-parts, who knew where the Internet revolution would lead?

When logging on, you are immersed at the center. As Kabir, the fifteenth-century Indian mystic poet, understood, "Wherever you are is the entry point." The Internet has no beginning and no end. No matter how long you migrate, no matter how far you navigate, you are at the center. You never reach the edge. You can be anywhere from where you are. It can feel like your imagination, except that it moves by mouse or track pad rather than thoughts (maybe someday!).

Metaphysically, everyone is born at the center. Yet, we mark our linear years with holidays, birthdays, anniversaries, vacations, and report cards. We define time by hours, minutes, and seconds. We live by days, nights, weeks, months, and years. We attempt to make life secure through our identities, age, position, and status. Sometimes, we try to hold on, especially to our youth. When we understand, however, that we are always at the center, perhaps we will stop trying to be somewhere else. Just be who we are at the center. Who we are.

The arrival of the Internet may be humanity's realization that all are accounted for, that everyone is together. The Internet belongs to all despite efforts otherwise. Everyone has access to all there is. Everyone can participate. We see the Internet and it is us.

Meanwhile, schools tend to stay with traditional curricula. In middle and high school there are separate subjects: English, math, social studies, science, foreign language, physical education, et al. Students feel they are being rushed and pulled from one class to another. But the Internet awaits, a vast resource to be explored. The field of cosmology with images on the Internet, the Hubble and the James Webb telescopes, awaits with a new creation story to be discovered. The images alone invite wonder, thought, and questions.

Why not take students through what scientists know about the origin of our universe? Invite them to ponder that everything is made up of atoms and, therefore, the universe is 99 percent empty—and so are they! Imagine them searching for their "emptiness."

The second big idea, which Edward Hubble discovered through his telescope in 1929, is that the universe is omnicentric with galaxies expanding away from each other in all directions. Images from the James Webb telescope may change that thinking.

Creation myths for generations have reflected on early human imaginations of our origins. These myths, appealing as they may have been, do not take into account what humans have come to know and understand about who we are and where we emerged from.

Cosmologists regard our planet as having been formed about 4.54 billion years ago from a third-generation star that provided minerals making up the periodic table. Would it not be wise to teach our children the story of this wondrous emergence, to tell the unfolding of the earth as we have known it? The James Webb telescope may alter that story. That's what science does.

Bill McKibben's concept of footprints, which focuses on the deleterious effects of climate change, opens an exploration of who we are and where we are headed. Taking his wisdom, excerpted here, you would do well to offer it to your students and open what should be intriguing conversations:

> Footprints, it's all about footprints.
>
> Given the exponential growth of the human presence, we live in a world that demands our full attention in order to survive. The ancients provided us with the power to create and savor as well as to dominate and destroy. We need to study them to learn how we came to create such large footprints on the planet. We need to learn their wisdom, a wisdom that can deepen and enlighten our consciousness and help us succeed on our planet. We are about to embark upon a wonderful adventure together—in class and hopefully on the earth in this special time in which we live.
>
> Enjoy the ride.[1]

Regardless of your subject matter, you should be aware of the origins of the universe and the human story on this planet as scientists now understand it. And if you act in ignorance, you may pass it on to your students. You are responsible for what you teach.

REFLECTION/ACTION

Reflect on the Internet as an extension of the human brain. Being "at the center" means it's true not only for you but also for your students. Think how understanding cosmology's insights into the evolution of the universe and of the earth can inform your teaching; ponder Bill McKibben's perspective. See yourself willing to be less linear and more open to ambiguity. Provide room for student rumination and generating thoughts. Pondering big ideas together can bring new insights and understandings for them—and for you.

Chapter 19

On Brain Research
Seek Applications for the Classroom

Teachers who implement proven brain research expand learning.

Brain research has had an unsavory history for schools. For example, the shoddiness of research behind "The Mozart Effect" and "Baby Einstein" caused teachers to steer clear of their claims. But you should not let such shams serve as an excuse to ignore viable brain research's well-documented information to assist you to become a better teacher in this fast-changing world. To ignore such resources, in some people's eyes, could be considered malpractice. Doctors, for example, must keep up with research to maintain their licenses.

If you want to transform your teaching, here are four exemplary examples.

Eric Jensen: A long-recognized practitioner, who has reached thousands of educators through books, conference presentations, and the web. His website provides instant downloads including his "10 Brain-Based Teaching Strategies," which provide proven principles to incorporate into the classroom.[1]

Tip seven of his 10 Most Effective Tips for Using Brain-Based Teaching and Learning advocates for more arts education in schools; Jensen cites the research of neuroscientists at five major universities, which confirm that the arts boost attention, working memory, and visual spatial skills, as well as social skills, empathy, timing, patience, verbal memory, and other transferable life skills.

The report adds that students gain the most value from the arts when they have classes thirty-to-sixty minutes a day three-to-five days a week. Not once a week for forty minutes—or in many schools only for a quarter of the year. Some schools have dropped the arts altogether in favor of core subjects and test preparation.

Jensen's compelling evidence about the role of the arts demands serious attention. Schools need to pay attention to his evidence.

John Medina: Author of the seminal book *Brain Rules*, Medina brings powerful ideas to energize classrooms. His *Brain Rule #1—Exercise* (*Exercise improves cognition*) is a case in point.

"Physical activity is cognitive candy," Medina writes.[2] Yet increasing numbers of schools have eliminated recess to provide more time for test preparation. Some schools do not have playgrounds.[3] Children need exercise!

What can a teacher do? Taking *Brain Rule #1* to heart, a teacher could try something like this:

- When students enter your classroom, you and they jog around the room for two minutes.
- When answering a question or making a comment, students stand (except during conversations).
- Students give high-fives to their neighbor when answering a question or having shared an idea.
- Students stretch before a quiz or test.
- Before leaving the classroom, students jog around the room together a couple of times.

David Sousa: His multiple-book collection on brain research, with its excellent "Practitioner's Corner" segments based on his classic *How the Brain Learns*,[4] is now in its sixth edition, post-Covid. His concept of "Primacy-Recency" deserves special attention.

According to Sousa, the best time to develop long-term retention—essential for education—begins at the front end of a lesson (Primacy); making time in the middle for students to process (Downtime); and the next-best learning time is in the closing minutes (Recency). In a forty-five-minute period, you can choose to do one Primacy-Recency lesson or two twenty-minute Primacy-Recency lessons.

Once you recognize the potential impact of Primacy-Recency, you can redirect your practice. Instead of beginning classes by covering the homework or launching into a lecture, you can begin a lesson with a mini ten-minute lecture, allow twenty minutes for students to process (in pairs or triads), and for the last ten minutes have students share what they learned.

Robert Greenleaf: His *brain-based workshops* invite teachers to rethink practice. Two ideas from his workshops help teachers do just that. The first, "Students are only as safe in your classroom as you are on your worst day."

It crystallizes the importance of having a safe classroom. "If a teacher loses composure with one student, the other students in the class will wait for their turn to receive a similar rebuke. It's difficult to undo the effects of rage, perhaps impossible."

The other quotation Greenleaf shares is from Elspeth Campbell Murphy: "If I were a student in my classroom, would I want to return tomorrow?" This powerful adage reminds you to pay attention to how your students are responding.[5]

This brief foray into the works of four brain researchers may encourage you to rethink your practice. Given the rapid change of expectations for schools in society, you will need all the help you can find. In today's digitally oriented society, those of you who have been in the classroom will have to reconsider how you taught in your first years, adjust, and perhaps radically change your approach. Brain research is no panacea but can help you become a more effective teacher.

REFLECTION/ACTION

Brain research is a challenging but valuable tool for you and your colleagues. Begin by searching the websites of Jensen, Medina, Sousa, and Greenleaf. Take time to dig more deeply into reading what they have to say. Perhaps form a reading group to encourage one another.[6] And explore brain research methodologies with your students.

Chapter 20

On Examining Practice
Provide Choices

*Frank's choice to be a "group of one" inspires
teachers to reimagine their teaching.*

At a faculty meeting:

The principle declares, "We'll break into small groups to discuss options."
"Why?" Frank responds, "Do you think we'll be smarter when we're in small groups?"
After bantering back and forth about the optimum group size, the principal gives in. "Fine! Just break into whatever size you think makes sense."
Frank decides to sit alone at a conference table.
"I like your style, Frank."
"Thank you for noticing," Frank replies.

Allowing a child, let alone a teacher at a meeting, to sit by himself. A strange option. Part of your job is arranging seating for your students. For those in elementary classrooms, it's often the choice of clusters with four or five desks pushed together. For middle school teachers, its often flexible small groups, while high school teachers likely give whole group lessons, often choosing to lecture to their students sitting in rows and columns.

However, in each of these situations, some students become restless. They seem unable to focus like their classmates. They distract others—and the teacher. They look away. They whisper to a classmate and even poke them. No matter what effort a teacher makes, their squiggling persists.

In the opening scenario, Frank's choice of where to sit was his choice. His principal listened and allowed him to sit alone. What if teachers adopted such an attitude with their students? What difference would it make?

Here's a thought experiment. You reflect on the past week in your classroom. You call up times when your teaching was challenged. Ryan, one of your favorites (only you know that!), spent much of his time fidgeting in his cluster. You try to keep him focused with his table-mates. But to no avail.

Imagine having taken a different tack: "Ryan, what's bothering you? Do you want to sit somewhere else?" Ryan immediately points to the empty desk in the corner of the room. You take a moment, a long moment, and then send him to that desk. He gathers up his materials and dashes over to the desk and quiets down for the rest of the morning. And you notice that none of the other students ask to be moved. You moved Ryan because you were concerned about him.

Taking time for thought experiments brings you to other observations. Perhaps your insistence upon cluster seating every day might not be such a good idea for your kids. And what happens with your other seating arrangements? Peter and Sam become calm when you read aloud, while George, Mary, and Veronica fidget more. During math, some seem to disengage while the others are into it, especially Ryan. The same type of pattern holds true for other situations. You realize that you should observe your students more closely in each arrangement to make your lessons more palatable. And you provide the right for your students to choose whenever possible.

Engaging in such thought experiments (after all, they were good enough for Albert Einstein!), invites you to become reflective about your teaching. Taking such time allows for surprising ideas to appear, for insights to arrive. As you enlarge your understanding of your classroom, you become more patient and more accepting of the challenges you face. More important, you see your students better able to learn. When sharing your thinking with your colleagues in conversation, you speak calmly, knowing of what you speak.

You decide to seek out other teachers as to how they arrange students. You discover that just down the hall, Ms. Kunhardt arranges multiple seating by putting chart paper on the board. She has one for each seating arrangement for students to follow; moving desks is quick and easy. You decide you will use her approach because of its flexibility.

All this thinking from learning about Frank choosing to sit alone. Keep your mind wide open, pay attention to what comes in, to what might show the way—the way in or the way out. Teaching at its best is full of surprises; new perspectives await.

REFLECTION/ACTION

Have you been willing to examine your practice to see what works and what does not? Have you been inspired by a colleague? Have you inspired one? Has a child "taught" you about your teaching, so much so that you've changed practice? And most important, have you opened your classroom to provide choices for students on what they do, what they say, and what they think? To be who they are. Try invoking thought experiments to see how they inform your practice.

PART IV

Letter Writing: The Power of Pause

*A thoughtful letter can bring pause to the bustle of
daily teaching life and provide encouragement.*

Years ago when a letter arrived in the mail—a rare experience today—we anticipated something important and often sat down before reading (unlike email!). Letters were that way for generations. When writing a letter, we would slow down, taking cognizance of each word. Our mind would pause, slow, reflect, and discover thoughts. There was no delete key. If we crossed out too often, we would begin again.

In the seventies in an open, multigrade middle school classroom, I chose to write letters to students instead of giving a final grade. I was in a school culture that had multiple teams of teachers, each one framing its own curriculum and grading procedures. In our team, I wrote letters in italic calligraphy at the end of the year in which I assessed each student's progress—and offered special encouragement for those moving on to high school. Throughout the year, I wrote interim letters to parents.

Later, as a consultant in the early 2000s, instead of only giving grades for professional development courses, I wrote email letters to each participant. While they lacked handwriting's personal touch, they were my effort to speak to each teacher to offer support and encouragement. I hoped they would try out the ideas and strategies we had generated together. And at the same time, I wanted to show respect for the daily challenges they faced. I found that writing to them encouraged me to reflect as much as to narrate. From my years in the classroom, I discovered hidden gems in the landscape of my mind. I gained as much from writing these letters as I hoped participants gained from reading them.

Choose to read the letters to Alicia, Pamela, and Peter one at a time. Reflect on each one and consider trying out the ideas you discover.

Chapter 21

Letter to Alicia

Celebrate Your Uniqueness

A consultant's letter of encouragement to support a new teacher's desire to hold on to her uniqueness inside an embedded traditional school culture.

Dear Alicia,

Your description of your first weeks of teaching is not surprising. You feel like you are being tossed about by encounters and challenges that you never anticipated. I do not know of any teacher who hasn't expressed similar feelings. I have some thoughts for you to consider.

What do you remember, Alicia, about one of your favorite teachers? Perhaps you felt her persona was hers alone, her style unique. No doubt, she cared about you and your classmates. She told stories around what she taught. You worked hard for her, and she worked hard for you. She may have seemed to know you better than you knew yourself. You likely felt welcomed every day and left each class with something to remember.

No doubt you recall other teachers who you felt were special. You and your classmates usually concurred on their good qualities. You likely agreed that they:

connected with you personally—or made every effort to;
taught you something to remember—at least you could feel their urging;
engaged you—hardly a lesson passed without posing intriguing questions or
 a perplexing problem;
surprised you—never seemed to settle into a rut;
had a sense of humor—and fit it into their teaching;
and knew you by name—and knew you well.

From our conversations, Alicia, you understand teaching to be a deeply personal pursuit. You understand that you are not simply replacing another teacher. You bring your special self. You say and do what no one else has ever done. You teach who *you* are every day.[1]

You have told me that you don't want to repeat what happened to you in many of your school classrooms. Every day the teacher stood up front, took attendance, made announcements, collected homework, delivered the lesson, assigned homework on the board—and you, you sat in an assigned seat and listened—most likely passively. The bell rung. You stood up and left.

You say that you want to create a classroom that is special, "one less traveled by." Yet, you are frustrated. Many of your students appear restless and standoffish. They seem disconnected. You see it in their posture. You notice it when they "forget" to do homework, despite your assignments being short and focused. Many do not look you in the eye. Sometimes it seems as if you are alone in the room.

Take time to see school from their point of view. For many, having been through Zoom and hybrid classes during the pandemic was discouraging. Having to isolate at home, and not being with friends was taxing. Allow for conversations as often as necessary to invite them to share their thoughts and feelings. They may be looking for ways to connect with you and have you connect with them. If, instead, you choose to "teach" without acknowledging the confused landscape before you, your lessons will pass into the ether.

You learned quickly that you are in a school culture that expects teachers to take care of their own problems. Still, you are not sure how to act when you face disorderly students. If you send them to the office, the administration may think of you as a poor teacher. Yet, if you do not find some way to constrain troubled students, you will be unable to teach. You signed a contract, after all, to be a teacher—and a good one at that. Asking for help was not part of the contract. You feel stuck. I suggest you consult with veterans in your department about how to cope with them. You may be surprised at what good advice you may find.

You have told me, Alicia, that you want to create a safe classroom with enlivened lessons. For example, if you have been doing routines like collecting homework after checking attendance, open instead by putting a provocative question on the board. Invite students to take a public position and stand under a sign in one corner of the room: "Agree," "Strongly Agree," "Disagree," "Strongly Disagree." Invite debate and encourage them to change corners if they change their mind—more than once if need be.[2] By standing up, their thinking is stimulated, especially for classes after lunch—something we know from brain research. There are countless ways to begin a class. By varying your pedagogy, students will arrive curious about what will be coming.

And here's another idea you can use after you have presented information. You can ask "What questions do you have?" instead of "Do you have any questions?" Try both and see what happens. You will be pleasantly surprised.[3]

You and your fellow new teachers are entering a new era, the vortex of a radical shift in our culture. Unless you respond with intelligence, creativity, and commitment, your students will zoom past you, ignoring your methods and approaches. With their digital tools they will find ways to educate themselves, as did pioneers who invented solutions to newfound problems. You will need to collaborate to create ways to nurture them to become good students, good citizens, and good people. This is not about indulgence. You have much to offer—and you need to decide just what that is.

One more piece to consider. When you step into your car at the end of a day, take a few moments to celebrate what worked, the successes you had that day, as small as they may have been. Perhaps an absent student returned to say she missed you. Another who had been difficult apologized for his behavior. Or the principal told you that she appreciated your upbeat attitude. Relish these moments—and look for them every day.

Finally, pay attention to how you are engaging with your students and who you are with them. If you don't, you will lose any chance of being their teacher. You didn't become a teacher to have that happen.

Sincerely,
Frank

REFLECTION/ACTION

Remember who you are as a teacher. Bring your best self to each class every day. When discouraged, seek the silver linings; they are there. And don't try to "go it" alone. Seek out colleagues, listen to your students, celebrate yourself, and remember you are part of a grand mission.

Chapter 22

Letter to Pamela

Make Partnerships Your Priority

A consultant's reflection on the importance of building strong partnerships with students as the foundation of good classroom management.

Dear Pamela,

I appreciated your getting in touch after all these years. You sound like you have enjoyed your teaching. Your letter has triggered a memory, which I'd like to share with you. It's been more than twenty years since I became a consultant and taught my first beginning-teachers class with you and your colleagues before the opening of school in late August. In preparation, my company provided packets for you, which incorporated ideas for good teaching based on research. Since then, I have had second thoughts about the focus of some of those workshops.

In one, the packet included Harry Wong's "formulas" (as I thought them to be at the time), formulas designed to develop a well-managed classroom—what Wong called "a well-oiled machine." He advocated that teachers establish rules, procedures, and routines before they attempt to teach. A well-managed classroom is essential, he emphasized, if students are to have any chance to learn. As I recall, Wong did not put stress on establishing good relationships. I wondered at the time if Wong's approach was incomplete but did not say anything.

Pamela, I stepped into my first classroom, now more than sixty years ago, and fully expected students to arrive ready to learn—or at least give me a chance to encourage them to. I hardly paid attention to rules and procedures. Perhaps, it was because I taught in an environment in which students and parents understood how to act in school. When students misbehaved, my colleagues and I dealt with them. Sometimes we kept them after school, physically intervened in disputes, occasionally sent them to the office, and sometimes called parents for a conference, who would back us up.

In my first year teaching ninth-grade European history, I based my lessons from the textbook on how I had been taught. I stood at the front of the room, assigned seats, took attendance, collected homework, passed out paper for quizzes and tests, shared information, asked questions, called on hands raised, administered bathroom and library passes, put information and assignments on the blackboard, injected humor, and passed back tests and papers. I knew my routine and so did my students.

In my second year, I moved to the eighth grade and my teaching paradigm shifted. My department head asked me to design an Area Studies course that would intrigue students. I dispensed with the textbook, designed my own lessons, and let go of most of my routines. Later, I taught in a progressive primary school in Oxfordshire, England, and returned to the United States to implement progressive practices in a fifth/sixth-grade team. My colleagues and I wanted to reinvent school as we knew it. I admit, had we known of Harry Wong's ideas, we might have been more articulate as to how to develop rules, procedures, and routines.

But, returning to reflecting on my workshops with you and your colleagues, Pamela, I believe the packet's emphasis on classroom management was not the right choice. I should have balanced that with my deeply held principle of the importance of connecting with students: knowing their names, their interests, their willingness to learn, their idiosyncrasies, their time in the district, etc., toward forming partnerships.

The more I think about it, I wonder if my emphasis on Wong unintentionally led you and your workshop companions to develop a mindset in which you may have stressed extrinsic controls rather than intrinsic approaches to help students learn how to gain control of their behavior.

Responding to my question, I feel it is doubly hard to answer. Students have endured the pandemic, Zoom and hybrid classes, and prolonged isolation. You are having to invoke creative responses. Judging from what I remember about you, you no doubt think of your classroom as a sanctuary where students can feel safe, understood, and cared for.

From what you've told me, your approach is to have a safe class with sensible parameters where you pay close attention to students. You value having conversations in partnerships with your students when setting up rules and procedures. At the same time, you expressed delight at being their teacher. You greet them by name at the door, ask about their lives, listen to their stories, and tell your own.

When students disrupt, I imagine you wait patiently and respectfully admonish only when necessary. You recognize that if you lose your temper, you will lose the respect of the class. To establish this balance is a challenge but essential for a successful classroom.

I imagine you extend relationship-building efforts beyond your classroom, in the halls, in the cafeteria, on the playing fields, at concerts and plays, and on the street and in shops. If possible, you make connections with future students and indicate how much you look forward to being with them. You might even hint, as I used to do, "I'm eager to get to know your mind."

Students pay attention to teachers' reputations just as you did in school. No doubt, Pamela, now that you've become a veteran teacher, you meet new students who already know about you—and you about them. You understand your reputation counts. You let students know from the first day that their place in the classroom depends upon a respect of themselves, their classmates—and of you. And you make clear your expectations for excellent work and for proper behavior.

You no doubt spend time, as well, processing their learning, including to listen well, speak respectfully, study hard, cooperate with others, and bring their best selves into the classroom. You care about who they are and who they want to become.

At any rate, I'd be interested in any of your recollections of our workshops—and of my reflections in this letter. I remember you as a mature, clear-headed young teacher who made an impact on your students from your earliest days. I hope when we discussed good classroom management that you had the wisdom to realize that it included being in support of strong partnerships with all of your students. At least, I hope somehow I had made that clear. I hope to hear from you again soon.

Sincerely,
Frank

REFLECTION/ACTION

How well do you remember your early days in the classroom? How do you see yourself differently today? How has the pandemic affected how you and your students are in your classroom? Do you do anything differently now? How does your classroom compare to Frank's impressions of Pamela's?

Chapter 23

Letter to Peter

Be Yourself

A coach's advice to a second-year teacher to prompt him to understand positive change in schools happens one teacher at a time.

Dear Peter,

You and I have talked a lot during these past two years. In our last conversation, you've expressed concern that many of your colleagues appear to pay more attention to what *they* are teaching rather than to what their *students* are learning. They seem to be more concerned with their *delivery* than with student *engagement*. You hear it in department meetings and at faculty meetings.

Why do you think many of your colleagues persist in teaching this way? Why do they stay locked into that paradigm? I have often wondered why it has perpetuated: a tyranny of the obsolete, ineffective, tiresome, stale, repetitive, outmoded, boring, monotonous, tedious, uninspiring, irksome, dreary, vapid, vacuous, banal, dull, dreary, and plain-vanilla patter of spewed sentence strings one class period after another—day after day, year after year.

Pardon my rant, Peter, but I have seen this dance at my desk in elementary school. I have listened to middle and high school colleagues say that daily lecturing prepares students for college. They have resisted alternative methods, because they think they would have had to slow down covering their material. Others are more comfortable facing students in order to keep their attention. They hesitate to use alternative groupings for fear of students becoming unruly and coming to the attention of administrators, who would conclude that they are poor teachers. By keeping control from the front of the room, they believe that they will have a better chance fitting into the school's culture—and having their contracts renewed.

Another topic you've raised recently concerns student apathy. Since the pandemic and students having been through Zoom and hybrid classes—and having been away from friends—it's no wonder many of them appear distant and disengaged. They have a malaise I've not seen before, a lack of energy, some even depressed. I'm impressed that you have taken time to listen to their concerns. And as you have done in the past, you do not deliver hamster-wheel-driven lessons talking at them from the front of the room for the class period, lessons that spin endlessly with no time for comprehension and understanding.

I don't mean to sound cynical. I know of many teachers who do their best to encourage student involvement; some are in your school. When they give lectures, they make them engaging with illustrations and anecdotes—and some provide intervals during class for processing.[1] They invoke a variety of learning formats including triads and pairs and provide opportunities for reflection. And they recognize that students have a wide range of learning preferences.

In the faculty room, you've heard a few veteran teachers complain about nearly everything. The biggest complainers, you've told me, are those who arrive just before school begins and follow their students out of the building at the closing bell. They treat teaching as if they're on a time-clock. They resist shifting to a new team or grade. They complain when asked to try new approaches, new curricula. "Oh, we've tried that, but it didn't work." "What I'm doing now is just fine." They prefer to do tomorrow what they did today and yesterday—an endless loop of mediocrity.

In other schools in which I have consulted, Peter—and this might surprise you—I often hear how highly the faculty and staff perceive themselves. They view their camaraderie, their *congeniality*, as evidence of their competence; I see this as a trademark of the profession.

However, faculties rarely move beyond social bonding to commit to *collegiality*, which requires them to focus on improving instruction. Spending time together developing and critiquing curricula and observing each other's classrooms. But teachers hold on to their privacy, which unfortunately assures that they can teach without anyone knowing what they are actually doing (except for their students)—a challenging paradigm to undo.

You and I have said, more than once, that teaching is not about feeling comfortable. It's about what happens to students. You have taken the courage to be yourself, especially as a second-year teacher. And you've had to accept that not all of your colleagues appreciate you.

I respect that you pursue your own ideas and do not retreat to do school as it was done to you. You are searching to find the real teacher within you. I know that you will persist and in the process, continue to discover through conversations the minds and hearts of your students—and for them to know yours. You understand the importance of partnering with your students.

As I have said to you and your fellow younger teachers, classroom change happens one classroom at a time. No amount of mandates will force teachers to teach differently. Only when principals and teachers decide to make changes do changes actually take place. I encourage you to continue to pursue your chosen path.

Sincerely,
Frank

REFLECTION/ACTION

What ways have you found to be yourself despite pressures to "fall in line"? Be sure to celebrate them. What ways have you considered to right the "wrong paths" in your school's practices? To confront your school's culture is challenging. If it becomes too painful, you may have to step away to find another school. Not easy!

PART V

Building Trust and Respect: A Plan for Better Schools

Making trust and respect the centerpiece of school culture assures that administration, teachers, and students succeed.

Given the hierarchical structure of schools, building trust and respect for all parties has been a challenge. Administrators are faced with having to comply with decisions from boards and state and federal authorities. Teachers, in turn, await decisions from administrators. And students in many classrooms follow dictates from teachers. And the politicians and parents are inserting themselves into schools.

The potential for democratic decision-making appears to be impossible. Building trust is off the table. Since the days of the one-room schoolhouse, American schools have had a hierarchical structure. Through the years, control from the top has been the watchword. The idea of progressive democratic schools surfaced briefly at times, but schools were quickly relegated to the top-down model.

The first chapter in this section argues for better and more thorough teacher preparation programs that make trust and respect the centerpiece of schools. The second chapter recounts America's evolution to the factory-model schools of today. And the third offers a new paradigm that schools should aim for. As with labor movements that succeed, it will be teachers who will lead the way. At least, that's the hope!

Chapter 24

See It, Say It, Fix It
Rethink Teaching

Involving all interested parties in decision-making enables trust and respect to emerge.

In the conclusion to his provocative book *How We Decide*, Jonah Lehrer shares how the aviation industry has practically eliminated pilot error.[1] Pilots take flight simulation training to encounter scenarios that threaten safe flights. The sessions engage their minds as well as their emotions to prepare them to react without thinking. No more listening to lectures.

Pilots follow up with training in Cockpit Resource Management (CRM). It teaches that during a crisis it is important to seek and accept a diversity of viewpoints. Instead of expecting the captain to have "God-like certainty," everyone in the cockpit is instructed to say what they think. Surgical teams in hospitals have instituted CRM. Lehrer cites the Nebraska Medical Center's mantra, "see it, say it, fix it" by which surgical teams have tripled the number of "uneventful cases," where nothing has gone wrong during an operation.

Lehrer depicts the pilot of the plane as its rational brain and the cockpit computers as its emotional brain. Both are necessary for successful flights. His description recalls Jonathan Haidt's metaphor of the rider and the elephant. In each person, Haidt describes, the rider (the mind or rational brain) looks out for possibilities while the elephant (the body or emotional brain) does what it has been trained to do.[2]

What might Lehrer's description of retraining pilots and surgeons have to do with teachers in schools?

Teachers work alone inside their classrooms in a strict hierarchical, factory-model culture. They are considered above paraprofessionals, secretaries, janitors, and kitchen help. Authorities at the federal and state levels, and school boards, superintendents, and principals frequently determine what is to be taught and when—and take control of year-end assessment tests. Within this framework, teachers are relegated to be purveyors.

Lehrer's explanation of the process to eliminate pilot error suggests a new paradigm for teachers. What if they were to participate in a CRM-like structure, in which they are included as equals at the decision-making table? What if "see it, say it, fix it" became embedded in school cultures, where teachers could speak freely about school matters without having to look over their shoulders? What if the culture of clout where higher-ups exert power becomes replaced by a democratic culture of mutual respect where everyone is listened to? Where conversation is central. Where trust and respect are at the center.

Would this new paradigm improve student learning? Yes, if schools chose to implement it. They could begin by initiating a "teaching-simulator" concept as part of teacher training—and for retraining (recertification). It would replace the largely lecture-based preparation combined with six-to-nine weeks of student teaching.[3] This concept can also be applied to professional development and education conferences, which traditionally involve presentations, frequently with PowerPoint slides.[4]

If this model were to work, teacher training will have to become more rigorous inside school settings. Following the medical profession's model, teachers begin their careers as interns. While they do not require as many years of preparation as doctors (the expertise is not as precise), they need more than they receive now.

Teachers need to work alongside master teachers and spend time observing in multiple classrooms, which approximates the grand-round process in hospitals. They should frequently reflect on their observations, write them down, and share them with colleagues. As they develop and teach lessons, they will receive constant feedback from master teachers and peers. And they should meet frequently with colleagues and each other for reflection and discussion.

Once teachers sign a full-time contract, they are given mentors to shepherd them through their first three years. Having a mentor assures them of acquiring a deeper understanding of how the school operates including scheduling issues, report periods, discipline of students, and evaluations among many others.

The rigor of this program would raise the level of the teaching profession. Candidates, who traditionally sought entrance into the profession as an easy path to employment, would learn the rigors of what it means to take full responsibility for a classroom. The training, internship, and close scrutiny of the candidate process will raise the bar for becoming a teacher. It will attract higher-level candidates and bring more respect to the profession. This process will take time. Perhaps teachers may even be given the title of "Teacher" like "Professor" in university and "Doctor" in medicine. A long shot.

At present, entering teachers are barely prepared yet are expected to teach a full load from the first day. No wonder half of them leave within five years. Until society chooses to treat teaching as a valued profession and invest wisely in its future practitioners, "pilot error" in the profession will not be corrected any time soon.

REFLECTION/ACTION

What are your thoughts about the present state of the teaching profession? Would you support the teacher preparation approaches offered in this essay? How do you feel about teachers being addressed as "Teacher." Is it realistic? And do you think there's any chance of improving compensation?

Chapter 25

Replace Factory-Model Schools
Eliminate Crippling Hierarchies

The lingering inertia of the factory-model school structure in the United States prompts important questions for the future.

We are into the third decade of the twenty-first century, yet schools continue to immortalize their factory-model origins. Despite the influx of innovative curricula, SMART Boards, computers, cell phones, and iPads, students often can be found with textbooks sitting at desks in rows in front of teachers like generations before them. Bells ring to signal the start and end of periods. Yellow buses deliver children from home to school and back.

So how did this model begin? Perhaps, from a conspiracy theory point of view, the scenario may have happened early in the last century. Leading industrial magnets, in a back room around a conference table, invoke the spirit of Frederick Winslow Taylor.[1] One of them offered a proposal:

Why don't we set up schools to prepare citizens to work in factories? We will design the buildings to mirror assembly lines. We'll make long straight hallways with rooms on each side. Each room will have children's desks set in rows and columns. We'll place the teacher's desk in front with a blackboard behind.

As we do in industry, we'll build the system from the top down. We'll hire men to be superintendents to organize each school and each classroom. They will hire other men to be principals to oversee each building. The principals will hire women as cheap labor to be teachers and place each one in a room where they will carry out the superintendent's plans.

We will assign children to grades based on their age. The superintendent and his board will determine the curriculum, textbooks, and the sequence of lesson plans. Teachers, in turn, will deliver these lessons and ask students to memorize and regurgitate the material. Each room will have a door with a clear-glass panel to enable the principal to check on teachers.

We will require children to attend what we'll call public schools. We will allow for those families who can afford it to send their children to private institutions, which we will endow. Public schools will select their best students to attend college or to train for professions, such as medicine and law. Families with means can prepare their children to pursue business interests.

The primary focus of the public schools will be to prepare children for the workforce. Here they will learn to accept authority, follow instructions, complete repetitive tasks, and know their place in society. They will be indoctrinated in the American way: loyalty first to factory, then to their family, to the community, and finally to the nation.

This hierarchical factory-model system remained in place throughout the twentieth century and now into the twenty-first century. Historical efforts at educational reform to break its rigid format have hardly made a dent. In the late nineteenth century into the mid-twentieth century, John Dewey and progressive education advocates made some impact on educational practice. It was not enough to subvert the factory-model system.

The Open Education movement in the 1970s, which grew out of England's Progressive Primary School movement, thrived briefly but also succumbed to the hierarchical structure of public schools.

A Nation at Risk, the 1983 report of President Reagan's National Commission on Excellence in Education, with its appeals for change, unfortunately, was an extension of hierarchical control of schools. George W. Bush's No Child Left Behind, and perhaps less so, Arne Duncan's Race to the Top during the Obama administration, continued the role of top-down directives. Betsy DeVos, secretary of education under Trump, worked to undermine the effectiveness of public schools by encouraging funds for charter and religious schools. The Biden administration under Secretary Miguel Cardona has begun to shift emphasis with reinvigorated funds for public education and support for teachers. However, the hierarchical system remains.

How can we overturn this system and, in its place, establish a new focus, giving teachers wide latitude to educate and make learning successful for each of their students? It can begin in the mind of each teacher.

Imagine the following scenario: You're a teacher. You take time before the first day of school and imagine yourself standing at your classroom door at the *end* of the school year. You visualize each of your incoming students departing from your classroom on their last day. You wonder what these students will become having spent a year in your classroom. You can't know, of course, but by asking questions, you can frame your focus on who you will be with them:

Who have they become being with me for the year?

How will they feel about themselves?
What have they learned and how will I know?
How well will they relate to each other having been together for the year?
What will they understand about themselves?
What will become important to them?
What will they value about themselves, about their friends, about their future?
What will they have learned to care about?
What difference will I have made with them?

These questions are but a sample that could swirl about in your mind. They indicate the deep complexity of the classroom and respect for the challenging work you do every day. They focus on intangibles, not on test outcomes. They open the need for conversations that provide feedback, both for you and for your students. And to extend this idea further, what if you invited parents to ask similar questions about their children in your classroom? To have them look ahead with you not only about how well their children will do but also who they will become.

What a shame if you feel pressure to comply with directives from authorities that determine the success or failure of your teaching; many of the "authorities" have never taught or have left the classroom so long ago that they've forgotten what it takes for teachers to succeed. And the pandemic complicated matters.

Successful teaching comes from years of responding to the above questions—and countless others. When asked about a former student, you will talk about who she was, not about her grades or test scores. Ask yourself if you would have decided to become a teacher if you had understood you would be forced to teach students how to take multiple-choice bubble tests and that these tests would determine their success—and yours.

In Jonathan Haidt's insightful rider/elephant metaphor, the rider represents the mind that looks around and conjures possibilities, sometimes exciting us to the point that we think we will immediately implement them. The elephant, on the contrary, reflects our habitual responses, what we've learned to do automatically to sustain our daily lives.[2]

We often underestimate the strength of our elephant. When, for instance, we see a film such as Frederick Wiseman's *Belfast, Maine*, which shames viewers into not eating fish, our "rider" swears to stop our habit. Three weeks later, our "elephant" has us eating grilled salmon.

Annual outside assessments assume that students and teachers are like Haidt's riders. You are told to deliver information that students are expected to absorb and then take tests to verify (usually on Fridays). Such testing assesses quick learning, often from memorization. Yet real learning, as represented by Haidt's elephant, takes time and persistence. To learn worthwhile knowledge, understanding, and skills requires commitment and practice. It includes invoking classroom conversations where students can explore and share their thinking in a supportive environment. Where they know who they are is more important than what they put on tests.

When authorities ask you to prep for multiple-choice bubble tests, they are depriving you and your students of the potential joy of discovering insights that emerge from thoughtful partnership. Your students are shortchanged when they believe that the quicker they "get it" the smarter they are, when those smarts are often ethereal at best. Knowledge memorized for tests is quickly forgotten.

When tests become the sole assessment criteria for success, the impact of your teaching will be relegated to the background. Test-driven teachers see students having labels stuck on their foreheads. Labels indicate scores from several days—in some cases weeks—of test scores and later of filling in bubble after bubble after bubble on outside assessments. However, you can choose to reflect instead on who your students will become throughout the year. No thought of placing labels on their foreheads.

You can decide to nurture your classroom's elephant. You can engage in teaching habits of mind that serve the greater good of each person and society. Through conversations, you challenge and provide support. You encourage preparation for an unknown future. And you pay attention to how each student is responding.

Teaching and learning is not a business. It does not seek to make a profit and construct a successful balance sheet. It is personal. It's about patience and persistence. It's about acts of love, in partnership with students to become who they are meant to become and how they can be of service to others.

If students are taught to regurgitate memorized moments, write formulaic five-paragraph essays, answer repetitive math questions, master dates from history, and memorize formulas in science, learning will, as my colleague Frank Gould said, "be like spitballs that cling to the wall without meaning."[3] Students will not acquire the necessary knowledge and thinking skills to participate fully in society.

And when you realize the tyranny of a hierarchical, dictated curriculum, and scores from outside assessments are largely determining the fate of schools, you should take it upon yourself to reverse this trend. You would be wise to invoke the words of Phillip Pullman:

> We should [not] give up and surrender . . . I think we should act *as if*. I think we should read books, and tell children's stories, and take them to the theatre, and learn poems, and play music, as if it would make a difference . . . We should act

as if the universe were listening to us and responding. We should act as if we were going to win.[4]

REFLECTION/ACTION

Do you agree that you and your fellow teachers are part of a hierarchical system that serves the interest of those in charge? What can you do to change this paradigm? Perhaps you can begin to make things happen your way behind your closed door. Feign conformity with the department and school and "do your thing" with your students. However, it has obvious risks.

Chapter 26

Invoke a New Paradigm
Make Trust and Respect the Centerpiece

> *When all parties have the courage to trust and respect each other, they make it possible for schools to become democratic institutions.*

In the twenty-first century, schools continue to focus on test score outcomes. Among the most demanding are the state and federal year-end tests. Teaching for success on multiple-choice bubble tests means bubble teaching, skipping from one bit of information to another to another. No time for lingering. No time for immersion. No time for thinking. And no time for cultivating partnerships. Preparing for these tests denies classroom time for having conversations to explore issues, pursue ambiguities, ponder perplexing problems, think about thinking, discuss pressing matters, and engage in important tangential conversations.

Meanwhile, schools perpetuate a fiefdom mindset, a self-driven, embedded isolated world that protects them from outsiders. Teachers hunker down behind closed doors in their private classrooms. Principals hole up in their offices, dealing with endless paperwork and mini-crises. Secretaries set up domains difficult to penetrate. Some parents feel intimidated when they come into schools; they may have had bad encounters as students, or they may fear being seen as inferior to teachers. But more recently, other parents storm into schools, making outrageous demands and threats. And students feel they are in fiefdoms, too, as schedules and rigid rules keep them separated from friends.[1]

The fiefdom mentality also exists between principal and teachers. Some teachers feel they have a natural right to decide who comes into their rooms, including principals, whether this provision is in the union contract or not—an ironic right to privacy in publicly funded schools.

Consultants feel this fiefdom mentality, too. Once when I was teaching a course on pedagogy to a school's staff, the superintendent asked me to visit classrooms to provide feedback on the strategies we had discussed. When an entrenched teacher, who distrusted the administration, declared in class that I could not visit his classroom, no one questioned his right; it was, after all, his fiefdom. A week later, I found a chance during recess to gently scale the walls of his "castle" and he "allowed" me to observe a couple of lessons.

As long as schools perpetuate the fiefdom culture, all parties—central office, principals, teachers, specialists, and parents—become susceptible to playing "the blame game" when matters take a downturn. Critics-of-the-moment step in and declare they know the causes of the failure and how to fix it. When other failures arise (as they inevitably do), new critics appear, establish their "credentials of the moment," and set the cycle in motion again. Efforts to reform succumb to pontifications rather than leading to real change. Social media only complicates matters.

Administrators and teachers need to come together and declare that the emperor has no clothes, i.e., look deeply into the failures of the hierarchical structure of schools and ask:

How can we break out of this embedded fiefdom culture?
How can we make the natural richness of teaching and learning become the centerpiece of education?
How can we become free to create and develop dynamic, exciting, enriching learning communities?
How can our schools and classrooms become first about the students, about each one of them?

The answer to these questions lies in what, upon reflection, should be obvious: *All parties in schools must commit to building a democratic framework of mutual trust and respect.* It will be hard work. It will take commitment. It will take time and patience. It will have to be grown. And it will demand frequent conversations allowing everyone to be heard.

As giving cannot happen without receiving, so it is true with trust. Reciprocated trust is mutual. Once they have it, people will want to be worthy of it. To build it inside hierarchical schools will take unwavering persistence and commitment. Invoking a democratic paradigm may appear impossible on the surface, but like great changes throughout history, it can emerge at any time with a few determined people.

Teachers need to take initiative. Teachers do not have to wait for someone to tell them to change practice. For example, a teacher recognizes that her students are not paying good attention to her lessons. She decides to look for better approaches. She opens her door to a colleague to receive feedback. In turn, the two of them encourage others to open their doors.

Developing trust takes time. The habit of teaching alone resides deep in teachers' psyche. Those who choose to collaborate discover that they learn more about teaching and become better able to respond to their students.

Teachers need to be receptive to new ideas and methodologies. Young children form habits of learning from kindergarten. Traditionally, by fourth grade most have internalized how to succeed in the school setting. Teachers who choose to form partnerships with their students pay attention to the contexts of their lives, and are aware of the demands of today's society. They are privy to how each of their students is negotiating today's digital culture, so different from theirs.

Teachers need to create and invent ways to meet digitally dependent students, more than halfway if necessary. It is essential to let go of outmoded traditional methods suitable for a different time and become open to approaches that will meet students' needs.

Professional development needs to become integral to the school day. Professional development, as with all professions, is essential. Traditionally scheduled only for two or three days a year, it should be integrated into the school's schedule. It needs to happen in the classroom as well as in faculty meetings.

Given that the pace of change is happening faster than ever, educators need consistent input and retraining to better meet today's students. They need coaching. They need opportunities for collaboration. And, they should determine what professional development will serve them.

Teachers need to open their classrooms to administrators. Teachers often manage to keep administrators at bay except for the required annual—and likely unproductive—dog-and-pony-show evaluations. However, they need supportive feedback from both administrators and colleagues. They form partnerships with principals and other administrators to observe everyday classroom activities, the teacher specifying what to look for. Such a change in the principal-teacher role will take patience from both parties.

Professional Learning Communities (PLCs), an important model, bring teachers and administrators together to meet regularly to collaborate on ways to improve teaching and learning.[2] PLCs, or approaches like them, should be in every school.

Teachers should elect principals. One of the fixtures in the hierarchy of schools is the school board's and the superintendent's appointment of principals to govern faculties. This act alone separates the principal from teachers and opens the potential for animosity. Having teachers elect, or at least approve of, the principal recognizes that both have a vested interest in each other. Trust and mutual respect from the beginning form the basis of a productive relationship.

Principals should acknowledge teachers as primary decision-makers. Effective leadership means that principals recognize teachers as primary decision-makers and agree to work alongside them and their students. And equally important, support and nurture collaboration throughout the school. Central office administration, too, must publicly recognize teachers as primary decision-makers and support principals in their effort to work with teachers.

Students, after all, deserve to have competent teachers who make it possible to realize their potential. Supporting collaboration improves teaching so that parents and students may no longer have the need to advocate for particular teachers, who they may perceive to be "the good ones," or to try to avoid those they think are "bad."

Evaluations should be democratic. Boards evaluate superintendents, superintendents evaluate principals, principals evaluate teachers, and teachers evaluate paraprofessionals. Inside a democratic paradigm of trust and respect, evaluations can come from where they best serve the persons being evaluated. Teachers evaluate each other; they evaluate administrators. Principals evaluate one another; central office personnel the same. Principals continue to evaluate teachers but from the point of view of forming partnerships rather than acting as authorities.

Teachers should initiate trust partnerships with students. Teachers can shift from treating students as receptacles to treating them as learning-partners. Conversation is the essential ingredient. Once teachers affirm this trust—which takes time and patience—they open their classrooms where students are free to engage. Teachers and students learn to accept struggle as essential to learning. They become collaborative decision-makers who recognize the value of persistence. Cooperation, not competition, becomes the watchword.

Student success belongs to everyone. Teachers understand that all students are the responsibility of every teacher. In a democratic paradigm, they are no longer left alone to deal with difficult students. Every teacher in the subject, grade, and team—and throughout the school—has a shared responsibility for students, and students know that every teacher cares for them. Such open collaboration of trust and respect builds confidence in struggling students.[3]

Because teachers focus on each student's learning potential, those who struggle on tests are not ignored nor relegated as "those who cannot learn," or viewed as products of bad teachers. They are provided the resources necessary to develop their full potential.

Establish school councils. Most schools have student councils. Administrations have committees, some are official, others ad hoc. Some schools have faculty councils, a judiciary committee, parent advisory boards. But democratic schools have a council that includes students, faculty and staff, and community members. A school council that invites all parties in the school community to come together to make policy enables conversation to be practiced at its best. It sends a message that all voices will be heard. Democracy (small "d") at its best.[4]

In conversations, all parties must listen to one another. Conversations need to be at the heart of every school. Listening begets listening. This means administrators listen to teachers without judgment. Teachers listen to administrators without assumptions. Teachers listen to students without interrupting. Imagine a school where people pay attention to each other as they do to a movie on the big screen. Alive with listening, classrooms become open to everyone's ideas. And so, too, with listening throughout the school.[5]

CONCLUDING THOUGHTS

Implementing a paradigm shift in schools, one built on trust and respect, will be daunting. Given their traditional hierarchical structure, some might argue that it's impossible. But it is essential if schools are to become twenty-first-century learning institutions in which teachers are able to provide students opportunities to develop competencies. The process begins with developing trust and respect of teachers that is acknowledged outright. With nonjudgmental support, teachers are free to do their best without having to look over their shoulder for rebuke or approval.

Inside a democratic paradigm, through conversations new initiatives raise expectations and assure greater excellence. No more covering up for teachers who hang on to their classrooms until retirement. No more exemplary evaluations of 90 percent of teachers in schools where half the students are failing.[6] Trust and respect will allow for full transparency.

The ideas offered here are but a beginning. When administrators and faculty choose to move into a democratic paradigm, they will discover new ideas and approaches. Schools, like individuals, have their personalities, their cultures. Administration, staff, students, and parents together in partnership can create through conversations democratic solutions that provide opportunities for everyone to succeed.

If schools fail to develop a democratically based system among all parties (including students), they will likely fall further into the sinkhole of striving for compliance to multiple-choice bubble tests that sort, select, and deny. Instead, each student should be nurtured for who he is becoming. Schools cannot afford, however, to waste anyone. It is not morally right.

REFLECTION/ACTION

Transforming hierarchical schools into democratic institutions will be a daunting task. But it can happen when beginning steps are taken. As a teacher, what can you do in your school to begin this process? Who can you engage? What risks are you willing to take? The road to creating democratic schools that reflect trust and respect among all parties is most challenging—but necessary.

Coda

Having schools in which all parties trust and respect one another is a high ideal, one that every school community should strive for. Until teachers become central in the decision-making process, they are vulnerable to criticism whenever anything goes wrong. Such blame leads to defensiveness and to more blame.

Conversations need to be at the center. When people are engaged in conservation, they are on an equal playing field. Everyone can speak, everyone listens. Through mutuality, ideas emerge. No one person has special access to the truth. In a democratic culture of trust, all parties work together toward solutions. When wrongs appear, as they inevitably do, everyone pitches in to fix them. Mutual respect takes commitment from everyone, from the superintendent to the maintenance staff. And it includes students.

Teachers, secretaries, paraprofessionals, guidance counselors, principals and assistant principals, deans, nurses, et al., when acting in partnership, serve to make a school function. Teachers, for their part, must respect the janitors who clean their classrooms, the cooks who prepare their food, the administrators who support them, and the students who sit before them. Without all of them, they would be unable to teach.

Understanding the dignity of each person happens through conversations and opens the door to remove the hierarchical structure of schools and replace it with a democratically based partnership of mutual trust and respect.

Notes

INTRODUCTION

1. I have had this Joseph Featherstone quotation since I attended a workshop with him in 1975 sponsored by I.D.E.A./Kettering Foundation. Featherstone is an advocate of progressive education, which was derived from the writings of John Dewey; it was revived in the English progressive primary school movement in the 1970s. Featherstone became one of the gurus of the open education movement in America. He continues to advocate for all children to have the right and access to a high-quality education. He is also well known as a poet and writer.

2. *Diplomacy* (Boston: Games Research, 1961).

3. See Frank Thoms, *Behind the Red Veil: An American inside Gorbachev's Russia* (Phoenix, AZ: SparkPress, 2020) for an adventurous account of the last days of the Soviet Union and about his being a teacher during them.

4. George Orwell, *Animal Farm* (New York: Harcourt, Brace and Company, Inc., 1946), 118.

CHAPTER 1

1. http:www.nsrfharmony.org. NSRF has created a five-day training program to prepare people to become certified CFG coaches.

CHAPTER 4

1. "10–2," http://pypteachingandlearning.weebly.com/uploads/1/3/9/7/13974650/10-2.pdf.

CHAPTER 5

1. I first learned of the term "gray kids" from Lavinia Ruiz, who was one herself.
2. Robert Kegan, *The Evolving Self: Problem and Process in Human Development* (Cambridge, MA: Harvard University Press, 1982), 15ff. (Italics mine.)
3. Personal conversation with Brian Flanagan and Carl Fitzgerald. Sadly, Brian died in July 2019 after suffering with Alzheimer's. I can still feel his vigor and energy and his love for his students and teachers.

CHAPTER 6

1. Quoted from the September 20, 2013, *Zippy the Pinhead* comic strip, distributed by King Features Syndicate.
2. Neil Gabler. "Constant Information—And Nothing Remembered," *Boston Globe*, November 26, 2009, http://www.boston.com/bostonglobe/editorial_opinion/oped/articles/2009/11/26/constant_information___and_nothing_remembered/. His reference to *Memento* refers to the 2000 film in which a man suffers from severe short-term memory loss.

CHAPTER 7

1. William Powers, *Hamlet's Blackberry: A Practical Philosophy for Building the Good Life in the Digital Age* (New York: Harper Collins, 2010).
2. Nicolas Carr, *The Shallows: What the Internet Is Doing to Our Brains* (New York: W. W. Norton & Company, 2010).

CHAPTER 8

1. *Julie and Julia* (Columbia Pictures, 2009). Sadly, Julie Powell died at the young age of 49.

CHAPTER 9

1. Margaret Wheatley, *Turning to One Another: Simple Conversations to Restore Hope to the Future* (San Francisco: Berret-Koehler, 2002), 29.
2. Ibid.

CHAPTER 12

1. Don Miguel Ruiz, *The Four Agreements: A Toltec Wisdom Book* (San Rafael, CA: Allen-Amber, 1997).
2. Ibid., 31.
3. Ibid., 48.
4. Ibid., inside front cover.
5. Ibid., 63.
6. Ibid., 70.
7. Ibid., from the book jacket
8. Ibid., 88.
9. Ibid., 100.
10. See the website https://www.thefouragreements.com/ for further information.

CHAPTER 13

1. These ideas come from Jon Kabat-Zinn and Thich Nhat Hanh.
2. Elissa Ely, "Slow Down and Take It All In," *Boston Globe*, May 30, 2010.
3. See Benjamin Hoff, *The Tao of Pooh* (New York: E. P. Dutton, 1982).
4. With thanks to Barbara Merritt for first sharing this story with me.
5. I first learned of this aphorism from Jon Kabat-Zinn in his talk at Bancroft School, May 1999.

CHAPTER 14

1. See Mary Budd Rowe in chapter 4, "On Lessons," about engaging students in large group instruction. Although her research occurred nearly forty years ago, her conclusions remain vitally relevant.

CHAPTER 15

1. Nikos Kazantzakis, *Zorba the Greek*. I received this excerpt from a friend early in my teaching. It can now be found on the web.
2. Thich Nhat Hanh, *The Miracle of Mindfulness: A Manual on Meditation* (Boston, MA: Beacon Press, 1987), 3–4.
3. Jennifer L. Roberts, "The Power of Patience: Teaching Students the Value of Deceleration and Immersive Attention," *Harvard Magazine*, November–December 2013.

CHAPTER 16

1. Edward Tufte, *The Cognitive Style of PowerPoint: Pitching Out Corrupts Within* (Cheshire, CT: Graphics Press, 2003). Now in its second edition, 2006.
2. Ibid., 4.
3. Walter Isaacson, *Steve Jobs* (New York: Simon & Schuster, 2011), 970.
4. Search Hans Rosling at www.ted.com.
5. Edward Tufte, *The Cognitive Style of PowerPoint*, 25.

CHAPTER 17

1. Laura Miller, "Far From Narnia: Philip Pullman's Secular Fantasy for Children," *The New Yorker*, December 26, 2005, and January 1, 2006, http://www.newyorker.com/archive/2005/12/26/051226fa_fact.
2. Brian Swimme and Thomas Berry, *The Universe Story: From the Primordial Flaring Forth to the Ecozoic Era—A Celebration of the Unfolding of the Cosmos* (New York: Harper Collins, 1992), 74.
3. Christopher MacDougall, *Born to Run: A Hidden Tribe, Superathletes, and the Greatest Race the World Has Never Seen* (New York: Vintage, 2011).
4. Carl Sagan, *Pale Blue Dot: A Vision of the Human Future in Space* (New York: Ballantine Books, 1997).

CHAPTER 18

1. Bill McKibben, "A Special Moment in History," *Atlantic Monthly*, May 1998.

CHAPTER 19

1. Eric Jensen at www.jensenlearning.com/.
2. John Medina, *Brain Rules: 12 Principles for Surviving and Thriving at Work, Home, and School* (Seattle, WA: Pear Press, 2008), 22.
3. According to Benjamin O. Canada, the superintendent of Atlanta schools, "We are intent on improving academic performance and you don't do that by having kids hang on monkey bars." See http://library.adoption.com/articles/no-recess-policies-being-implemented-in-u.s.-school-districts.html.
4. David Sousa, *How the Brain Learns* (Thousand Oaks, CA: Sage, 2001), now in its sixth edition (2022). The other books in this series, also from Sousa, include: *How the Brain Learns to Read* (2004); *How the Gifted Brain Learns* (2002); *How the Special Needs Brain Learns, Second Edition* (2006); *How the Brain Learns Mathematics* (2007); *How the ELL Brain Learns* (2010); and *How the Brain Influences Behavior: Management Strategies for Every Classroom* (2009).

5. See greenleaflearning.com to explore options. See also his handout PDF: http://greenleaflearning.com/Documents/Handouts/Web_Brain_Handouts_Greenleaf.pdf.

6. Serious students of brain research may want to read the National Academies of Sciences, Engineering, and Medicine's *How People Learn II: Learners, Contexts, and Cultures* (Washington, DC: The National Academies Press, 2018). This work remains the definitive compilation of brain-based thinking. One has to be committed to study it.

CHAPTER 21

1. See Parker Palmer, *The Courage to Teach* (Hoboken, NJ: Jossey Bass, 2007) for a comprehensive understanding of the idea that we teach who we are.

2. Thanks to Margaret Caldwell, Hanover High School, Hanover, New Hampshire.

3. Ted Thornton made this important distinction at my faculty workshop at Northfield Mount Hermon School, January 5, 2011.

CHAPTER 23

1. See Mary Budd Rowe in chapter 4, "On Lessons," about engaging students in large group instruction. Although her research occurred nearly forty years ago, her conclusions remain vitally relevant.

CHAPTER 24

1. Jonah Lehrer, "Coda," in *How We Decide* (New York: Mariner Books, 2009), 251–59.

2. Jonathan Haidt, *The Happiness Hypothesis: Finding Modern Truth in Ancient Wisdom* (New York: Basic Books, 2006).

3. Notable exceptions are programs such as the Upper Valley Educators Institute (UVEI) in Lebanon, New Hampshire; the Teacher Training Course (TTC) at Shady Hill in Cambridge, Massachusetts; the New Teachers Collaborative at the Francis W. Parker School in Devens, Massachusetts; and the Newton Public Schools' Teacher Residency Program in Newton, Massachusetts.

4. See chapter 16, "On PowerPoint," for more information about its detrimental effects on learning.

CHAPTER 25

1. http://en.wikipedia.org/wiki/Frederick_Winslow_Taylor.

2. Haidt, *The Happiness Hypothesis*.

3. Personal correspondence.

4. Miller, "Far from Narnia: Philip Pullman's Secular Fantasy for Children," 3.

CHAPTER 26

1. Michael Schmoker articulates a "buffer zone" concept for schools that led me to describe fiefdom domains. See Michael Schmoker, "The Buffer," ch. 1 in *Results Now: How We Can Achieve Unprecedented Improvements in Teaching and Learning* (Alexandria, VA: ASCD, 2006), 13–22. Thanks to Chet Kozlowski for coming up with the term "fiefdom," which he derived from my writing.

2. The Professional Learning Community reform effort led by Richard and Rebecca DuFour has demonstrated an effective way for teachers and administrators to work together to focus on students learning. Solution Tree is the best resource at: http://www.solution-tree.com/Public/Main.aspx.

3. See chapter 5, "On Recruiting" for an expansion of this essential idea.

4. Hanover High School, Hanover, New Hampshire, instituted its school and community "Hanover High Council" in 1977, which continues to this day. See https://council.hanovernorwichschools.org/.

5. For a lucid description of the power of listening, see Rebecca Z. Shafir, *The Zen of Listening: Mindful Communication in the Age of Distraction* (Wheaton, IL: Quest Books, 2000), 81–102.

6. Meg Campbell, "Grade Inflation for Boston Teachers?," *Boston Globe*, May 24, 2013. Meg Campbell points out the discrepancy that 92 percent of Boston teachers who were evaluated received proficient or exemplary ratings, while more than 50 percent of Boston students were failing.

About the Author

Frank Thoms was a classroom teacher and consultant for fifty years. Now, as a writer, he devotes himself to improving the teaching profession to meet the challenges of today's digitally wired, techno-literate students.

Frank has taught in public and private schools in the United States, as well as in schools in England, Russia, Kazakhstan, and Mexico. He is a founding member of the Upper Valley Educators Institute, one of the nation's first alternative teacher certification programs, now in its fifth decade.

In the 1970s, he developed a model open-education classroom that served as a resource to New England schools. He has consulted for PBS, AFS Intercultural Programs, the Boston area teachers' exchange, the Kettering Foundation, the Association of Independent Schools in New England (AISNE), and the Vermont state Department of Education.

As a consultant, Frank served in more than 125 schools, providing keynotes, workshops, pedagogical courses, mentoring, and teacher coaching. His unique style blended serious content and pedagogies in an interactive format that served as a model for the kind of teaching he advocates for throughout this book. You can find out more about Frank at frankthoms.com.

www.ingramcontent.com/pod-product-compliance
Lightning Source LLC
Chambersburg PA
CBHW032028230426
43671CB00005B/238